Library of
Davidson College

VOID

Rush versus harmonic growth

PROFESSOR DR. F. DE VRIES LECTURES

RUSH VERSUS HARMONIC GROWTH

Meditation on the theory and on the policies of economic growth

JÁNOS KORNAI

*Professor of Economics
Institute of Economics
Hungarian Academy of Sciences*

1972
NORTH - HOLLAND PUBLISHING COMPANY
AMSTERDAM – LONDON

© *North-Holland Publishing Company, 1972*

All rights reserved. No part of this publication may be reproduced, stored in a retrieval system, or transmitted, in any form or by any means, electronic, mechanical, photocopying, recording or otherwise, without the prior permission of the copyright owner.

ISBN: 0 7204 3407 6

PRINTED IN THE NETHERLANDS

CONTENTS

Introduction		VII
Foreword		IX
1.	Background: problems of Hungarian economic growth	1
	1.1 Preparation of the first Hungarian long-term plan	1
	1.2 The basic dilemma	4
2.	Notion of harmonic growth: first approximation	9
	2.1 The factors shaping the requirements of harmony	10
	2.2 Internal information	13
	2.3 External information: international main streams	15
	2.4 Circumspect use	20
3.	Requirements of harmonic growth	25
	3.1 Preliminary remarks	25
	3.2 Twelve requirements	29
	3.3 Polemics and delimitation	51
4.	How to measure harmony	61
	4.1 A single indicator?	61
	4.2 Indicators of 'flow' and 'stock'	62
	4.3 Sacrifice – postponement – neglect	67

	4.4 The front-line of progress	76
5.	A special type of disharmonic growth: rush	81
	5.1 The factors of speed	81
	5.2 Diversity of the disharmonic paths	84
	5.3 The 'pure' type of rush	87
	5.4 The causes and motives of rush	90
	5.5 Harmony and the rate of growth	93
6.	Hungary in transition from the disharmonic to the harmonic path	99
	6.1 Meeting of the harmony requirements: the twelve requirements	99
	6.2 Satisfying the requirements of harmony: summing up	114
	6.3 Transition and the rate of growth	117
	6.4 Transition and the standard of living	123
7.	Disequilibrium	127
	7.1 The investment tension	128
	7.2 'Suction'	131
	7.3 Digression: polemics with the theory of 'unbalanced growth'	136
	7.4 Reserves and adaptation	137
8.	Effect of the plan and the market on the harmony of growth	141
	8.1 Division of labour	141
	8.2 Interrelation of reforms and change	144
References		147

INTRODUCTION

Professor János Kornai, who is chief of department at the Institute of Economics of the Hungarian Academy of Sciences, and who was visiting Professor in Great Britain and the United States, has become well known for his work on multilevel planning: not only for its contents, but also for the clarity of exposition. Having been invited to give the F. de Vries lectures during the spring of 1971, he chose to deal with some problems of long-term or perspective planning. Again his contributions constitute a number of original ideas of importance to any type of research on the future. The Directors of the F. de Vries Foundation feel that they serve the purpose of the Foundation, that is, to honour the memory of the great Dutch economist in an excellent way and they are happy to publish the remarkable lectures given by Professor Kornai.

J. Tinbergen
Chairman, Board of Directors

Professor F. de Vries (1884–1954) became the first professor of economics at the Netherlands School of Economics (Rotterdam), which was founded in 1913. In 1945 he accepted an offer of the University of Amsterdam to teach economics in its Faculty of Law. On the occasion of his 70th birthday, May 2, 1954 his pupils created the Prof. F. de Vries Foundation to honour a most influential teacher and a scholar of outstanding theoretical and practical wisdom.

The aim of the foundation is regularly to invite prominent economists from abroad for a series of lectures on theoretical subjects, as a stimulus to theoretical work in economics in the Netherlands.

FOREWORD

I am grateful to the 'Professor de Vries Foundation' for honouring me with its invitation which gave me the opportunity to expound my ideas on the problems of harmonic growth.

The Netherlands are a stimulating environment for discussing planning and growth. Dutch economists have played an epoch-making role in developing planning theory and in working out the econometric methods of planning. Though I was not fortunate enough to study in Holland, it will not count as immodesty if I declare that, on the basis of having studied his works, I consider myself, together with several of my Hungarian colleagues, a disciple of J. Tinbergen.

I take the opportunity to thank my hosts for their attention which made the days of my stay in Holland so memorable.

With some additions, my study comprises my lectures given in Rotterdam in April, 1971. It reflects the informality and looseness usually allowed in an oral presentation. I do not consider it a theoretical work in the stricter sense, rather a linking up of some ideas, a meditation on the exciting problems of economic growth. The study does not pretend to cover every important problem of growth, it restricts itself to a few questions, taken out of their context. Even these will be examined merely from the economic viewpoint, and a deeper political and sociological analysis will be left to later works.

I should like to thank in this place Mr. G. Hajdu and Mrs. H. Bliss who helped me in editing the English text of my lectures.

Conversations in both Rotterdam and Budapest held out the promise that the study might release fruitful discussions, even in its present unpretentious form. I must make further efforts in research to achieve more mature theoretical results.

Budapest — Rotterdam, 1971.

J. Kornai

CHAPTER 1

BACKGROUND: PROBLEMS OF HUNGARIAN ECONOMIC GROWTH

1.1. Preparation of the first Hungarian long-term plan

What I have to say is based mainly on the experience I have gained in the course of studying the development of the *Hungarian* economy.

During the last quarter of a century six medium-term (usually three- or five-year) plans were worked out in Hungary; the sixth is now under implementation. At the same time, the country's first long-term, fifteen-year plan is in the process of being drawn up. Hungarian planners have no satisfactory practice in long-term planning and thus the venture can be justly regarded as a pioneering one under our conditions.

A great number of Hungarian economists participate in the work with vivid interest. Nine committees and several sub-committees have been formed, comprising hundreds of members. Men of theory and practice equally take part: professors and enterprise managers, research workers of academic institutes and planning specialists of the Planning Office and the Ministries. I have the honour of being a member of the Economic Committee of long-term planning, called upon to give advice in general economic problems.

Many thousands of pages have been already written. Some of them have been published in periodicals, some serve as information for those participating and those taking political decisions, in a duplicated form. All this vast mass of material served as one of the main sources of this study, and that in a double sense*.

---

* It would be impossible to list the authors of all the works from which I have learned. I mainly stress those from whom I have borrowed particularly many ideas or data:

E. Ehrlich, F. Jánossy and J. Timár: National Planning Office and the Institute of Economic Planning; R. Hoch, J. Kovács and J. Rimler: Institute of Economics, Hungarian Academy of Sciences.

Thanks are due to some leaders of the National Planning Office, to Deputy Chairmen, J. Drecin and I. Hetényi, and to G. Darvas, Head of Department for Long-term Planning, who called my attention to many an important interrelation in personal interviews.

I lectured on some of the main ideas of this study in a Seminar of the Planning Office, and the discussion taking place there helped to clarify my ideas.

The first draft of my study has been read and commented upon by several of my colleagues. Beyond those already mentioned – all of whom helped me in correcting the draft – particularly the remarks of M. Augustinovics: National Planning Office; T. Bauer, G. Cukor, I. Friss, A. Madarász, B. Martos and T. Nagy: Institute of Economics, Hungarian Academy of Sciences, have been instructive.

Partly, I have taken over many ideas expressly from these documents. Partly, the materials on long-term planning reflect the discussions of the Hungarian economists: their differing and, at times, even conflicting views. Following their discussions had a stimulating effect on the development of my own point of view*.

It follows from the above remarks that I cannot claim to be original in every respect. I would be satisfied if I could give an impression of what is now 'in the air' in Budapest, among those drawing up the long-term plan. But even if much of the thoughts and the numerical material have been 'borrowed', the *selection* from among the many kinds of (and perhaps conflicting) views, from the millions of data, is necessarily arbitrary and subjective; the *system* of ideas expounded in the study is individual. In the light of the documents on long-term planning I have made efforts to explain and develop such ideas of mine which have been engaging me for fifteen years – ever since I started my scientific investigation of planning and economic policy. Finally, I have developed ideas for which I alone can be held responsible. I am not going to review some 'official Hungarian standpoint', – the less so, since at the time of writing this study no

---

* Some papers on the problems and methods of Hungarian long-term planning: M. Augustinovics (3) and (4), G. Cukor (12), I. Hetényi (22), (23) and (24).

valid decision existed on the estimates of the fifteen-year plan*.

Studying the materials of long-term planning has proved to be instructive for the theoretical economist from a further point of view. It has shown to what extent theoretical achievements are really usable and workable for practical planning, and in what respects theory appeared to be empty, floating in the air without support, or, for that matter, even misleading. My study tries, at several points, to confront the real problems, difficulties and questions of long-term planning and economic policy with the theories of various economic trends and schools and, if necessary, enters into polemics with the latter.

1.2. The basic dilemma

If psycho-analytical tests could be performed on long-term planners and the theoretical economists involved in planning, the symptoms of a peculiar *plan-schizophrenia* could be discovered: they seem to have two conflicting souls.

Soul number one is the 'harmony-soul'. This soul of ours is anxious and nervous in view of the disproportions and imbalances in the economy. It would like to make the idea of harmony into the core of the long-term plan. Our main task is to bring order into

---
* Collection of material for the study was closed in July 1971.

the country; to straighten the front-line of economic progress, to raise the relatively backward activities to the level of the forward rushing, pioneering performances.

A man who wears a shirt made of fine material, a beautiful tie, an elegant jacket, but worn, though acceptable, trousers and, in addition a pair of shoes with holes in their soles, makes a disharmonic impression. 'Soul number one' would like every piece of our clothing to be more or less of the same standard: perhaps we should have a shade less fine, more modest shirt and jacket, but also flawless shoes.

Soul number two is the 'growth-rate soul'. This soul of ours is enthusiastic above all for a fast and still faster rate of growth.

The growth rate is a fetish of our times*. It is a well known fetish in Moscow and Washington, in Tokio and Peking — why should it be unknown in Budapest?

Apart from minor fluctuations, the growth rate was stable in the past two decades: 5.7 per cent in the average of the years 1950-1969. On average for the years 1950-1959 the annual growth rate of national income was 5.9 per cent, in the period 1960-1969 it fell to 5.5 per cent**.

---

* Insofar as here and in the following the 'growth rate' will be mentioned, in general terms, without any qualification, we mean by the term the rate of growth of some aggregate index number of output (GNP or GDP or national income). It thus relates to some index number of *production*, not of consumption or of the stock of national wealth.

** See the publication (72) of the Central Statistical Office, p.68.

This is not a bad performance in itself, but growth is faster in many other countries. From among the socialist countries, the rate of growth is higher in Rumania or Poland; from among the capitalist countries, however, it is higher not only in Japan, but recently also in Spain or Greece. The 'growth-rate soul' harbours a competitive spirit and that objects to growing slower than other countries. It demands that the acceleration of the growth rate should be the main objective of the long-term plan.

We have mentioned two requirements. Do the requirements of harmony and of accelerating the rate of growth contradict each other? Many an economist will answer negatively: the case is just the reverse! Fast growth is precisely an indispensable condition for eliminating disharmonies, disproportions. A faster growth of national income creates the resources with which the development of more backward branches and activities can be promoted.

I for one, cannot agree with this line of reasoning. I am convinced that we have here really two requirements which, to a certain extent, contradict each other. This conflict will be the main subject of my study. To clarify the problem, the following questions will have to be discussed:

— The criteria and requirements of harmony.
— Special features of Hungarian growth; the disharmony and disproportion appearing in our economy.
— Interrelation between harmony, disharmony and

the rate of growth. Conditions and consequences of shifting from a disharmonic path to a harmonic one. — The roles of planning and the market in creating and maintaining harmony.

CHAPTER 2

NOTION OF HARMONIC GROWTH: FIRST APPROXIMATION

I use the term 'harmony' many times in my study — without being able to give a satisfactory definition for the notion. This requires further research. At the present stage of my knowledge I am compelled to restrict myself to suggesting the notion: I will circumscribe in several steps what I mean by harmony.

Harmony is a possible property of economic growth, which, however, does not assert itself necessarily in every kind of growth. It is dynamic interrelation among the various partial processes of growth which satisfies certain *requirements of harmony*. The requirements themselves will be treated later, in chapter 3. Firstly, however, I shall attempt to approach clarification of the notion of harmony in a somewhat more general form.

2.1. The factors shaping the requirements of harmony

First of all, let us examine the factors that are shaping the requirements of harmony (to be reviewed in detail in chapter 3). I will stress four factors.

(1) Human needs are many-sided. True, there may be great individual differences. One man will live in penury half his life to make a really great voyage at the end of it, the other will subordinate all his expenses to the delights of the table. But, even with the addicts of these extreme passions, the diversity of needs appears: each of them has to live somewhere; must be clothed, travel, etc. And what matters are not only the lowest threshold values of the various groups of needs — which are determined biologically, and even more socially. It can be observed as a stochastic mass phenomenon (and since Gossen this is not unknown to economists) that people strive, under the effects of social influences, to satisfy their needs proportionately, on a level corresponding to their environment, their material and cultural circumstances. If they reach a higher standard of living, they claim better quality food, more cultured living quarters, more comfortable transportation — all at the same time. We have general rules of human nature, of the development of needs, the concrete forms of appearance of which depend on the prevailing social circumstances.

The requirements of harmony reflect in the first

place the rules of proportionality among human needs.

(2) The second factor shaping the requirements of harmony is of a technical nature and relies on rules of natural sciences and on engineering experience. I think of the well known technological relationships between the inputs and outputs of production. It is upon these technological relationships that the technically determined phenomena of complementarity rely: e.g. the number of cars, the road network and the network of gasoline pumping stations must grow together in determined proportions, since each of these are indispensable inputs of motorized transportation.

(3) A further factor shaping the requirements of harmony is the effort of economic leaders and engineers at rationality, at an efficient and economic use of resources.

(4) Last, but not least: political and ethical considerations also play a role in shaping the harmony requirements. Hungarian planning terminology usually calls this factor 'state preferences'. The political bodies responsible for the control of society cannot look neutrally at the development of the structure of needs, but interfere with it. E.g. in order to spread culture financial support is given to publishing, to the cinemas, to theatres, to musical life. There are some free or very favourably priced services to promote the greater use of social resources to serve the education and teaching of children than would be destined for the same purpose by isolated individuals.

The four factors listed can be strictly distinguished from each other only on an abstract level. The first and the second assert themselves — using Marx's term — in a 'natural' (naturwüchsig) way, while the third and the fourth factor express conscious efforts relying on normative considerations. In reality, however, the factors appear interlinked, mutually affecting each other. The statistically observable input–output relations have been formed under the combined effect of blind technical necessities and of decisions aiming at efficiency and rationality. The pattern of consumers' demand is simultaneously influenced by general psychological and special socio-economic factors, as well as by measures of government economic policy.

From what has been said, some general conclusions can be drawn for understanding the notion of 'harmony'.

'Harmony' is not a purely objective category free from value judgement. Though in its quantification we may rely on empirical observation (this will be dealt with below), it is necessarily interlinked with normative requirements. However desirable it might be to distinguish sharply and logically the objective 'must' from the subjective 'it would be fine, if . . .' — this seems insoluble when speaking about the harmony or disharmony of economic growth in some country.

Another general conclusion deriving from the survey of the four factors: there are no harmonic proportions that would be valid once and for all, at any time and in every country. On the one hand, the concrete requirements may differ *by countries*, depending on the natural and social endowments of the different countries. On the other hand, the requirements change *over time*, and in a double sense at that.

In the course of its history a country follows a path of economic development. Now, requirements of harmony are different in a country just emerging from backwardness from those prevailing in another one which has attained a high stage of wealth.

Beyond that, the requirements of harmony change also with the historical calendar. From a moderately developed country (say, with a per capita GDP of 1000 dollars) a different structure can be demanded in the name of harmony in 1920 from that to be asked half a century later, in our days.

Harmony is thus a *dynamic* requirement. It is incompatible with rigid proportions among various sectors, various economic activities, but demands proportions shifting with time according to definite rules.

2.2. Internal information

The requirements of harmony are 'tangible' but hard to grasp, although some points can be found to hold on to when wrestling with the concrete formulation and quantification of the requirements. These points can be classified into two main groups: *internal* (domestic) and *external* (international) signals, information, data.

One of the most important internal sources of information is the price system. There exists a vast theoretical literature discussing how resource allocation can adjust to consumer preferences by relying on the signals of an ideal price system. I must confess, I feel many doubts both about the scientific methodology and the theorems of this literature about the general equilibrium theory and the interrelated neoclassical price theory. But I have explained this in another work of mine* and I would not like to get entangled in the complexity of the problem here. I would rather remain on a more practical level: an outline of the Hungarian situation.

We may obtain signals about the infringement on the harmonic ratios of needs (be it either consumer or producer demands) from the shifts in relative prices. The effect of lasting equilibrium disturbances on prices can be felt particularly where prices are free or relatively less subject to regulation. Even if there were no other indications, we would perceive that the production of the construction industry is lagging behind the demand raised by the other branches from the very fact that in recent times building prices have risen much above the rise of the general price level.

Disproportions may be indicated by dwindling or

---

* This is one of the main subjects of my book 'Anti-Equilibrium' (42), (43) published in 1971.

accumulating inventories; the buyers 'queue up' before sellers, unsatisfied orders are accumulating.

And finally, we may acquire information about disproportions, disharmonies also by hearing the direct objections: the 'grumbling' of the housewife, if she cannot get something in the shops, the complaint of the urban dweller about the lack of water in summer, the angry words of drivers about neglected roads, etc. And, as a matter of fact, these are mild forms of protests; in worse cases dissatisfaction may be expressed in much sharper forms — in strikes or demonstrations.

It is a common characteristic of all the signals listed — the shift in relative prices, changes in inventories, 'grumbling' or other protests — that they are *ulterior*, and, in a considerable part, of *negative* character. They impart information when those immediately interested perceive the disharmony. This is very important and a good economic policy must not leave even mild warnings unheard lest graver frictions should emerge. It is, however, worth while complementing the ulterior signals with *anterior* ones, the negative signals with *positive* ones. The main source of these is international experience.

2.3. *External information: international main streams*

In the development of every country there is something individually specific, which is historically irreproducible. It is certain that Hungary – say, when attaining the 1200 dollar/capita level – will not copy the state on this level of either Czechoslovakia or the Netherlands. Still, there are partial interrelations which show definite international regularities.

Let us have a simple example. In fig. 1, the horizon-

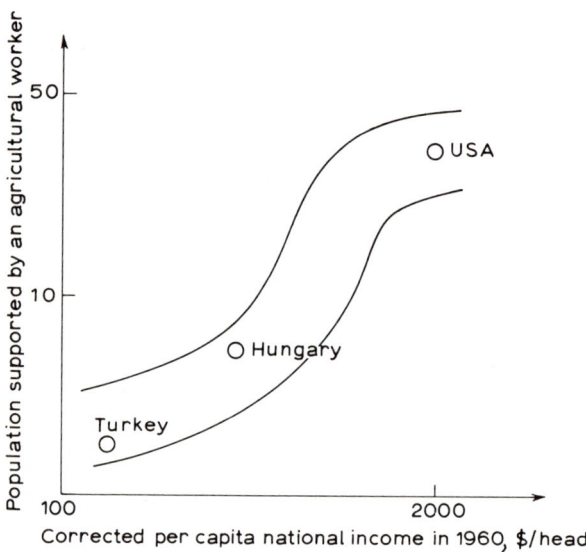

Fig. 1. Population supported by an agricultural worker as a function of the level of economic development.

tal axis represents a general indicator of economic development level; the unit of measurement is the so-called 'corrected national income, dollar per head'*. On the vertical axis we find a quotient: total population devided by agricultural employment (corrected for the balance of trade). The author of the figure fitted a regression line to the data of 21 countries; more exactly a band, the enclosing curves of which run parallel with the regression line, above and under it. The data of almost every country can be found within the band. It can be observed that the number of inhabitants 'kept' by agricultural workers — supplied with food and other agricultural products — grows as a function of general economic development level. Development is first slow, then accelerates and slows down again. In the figure we can find the place of Turkey at about the beginning of the band, and that of the USA at the end of it. As can be read from the figure, in respect of this indicator Hungary,

---

* The source of the figure is the study (17), (18) by E. Ehrlich. Also in later parts of my study I will frequently refer to the international comparisons of F. Jánossy, E. Ehrlich and Z. Bekker. The methodological bases of these researches were worked out by Jánossy. I will neglect their detailed description; the reader may find them in the work by Jánossy. See (31) and E. Ehrlich's papers (15), (16) and (19). I will make only a single explanatory remark. In fig. 1, and in some similar figures reproduced in my study, the horizontal axis shows *not* the standard notion of national income as used in economic statistics. The Jánossy method draws conclusions on the level of economic development from the constellation of a great number of physical indicators (e.g. stock of telephone sets, of cars, the consumption of paper and of electric energy, etc.) and from international cross-section and time series analyses of such similar indicators. The '*corrected* national income, dollar per head' on the horizontal axis is the measure of 'general economic development level' calculated in this manner.

moderately developed as she is, can be found to be in the main stream of international development.

In the following the term will be repeatedly used to denote interrelations similar to those illustrated in fig. 1: *the historical main streams of world economic development or, briefly, the main streams.*

There are interrelations, economic indicators, in which no such main streams can be observed; the international cross-section and time series data are so dispersed that we cannot read any marked regularity from them. In many cases, however, we can discover quite obvious international historical regularities, which can be well used in planning.

In connection with the notion of 'main stream' attention must be called to some qualifications.

(1) The main stream always indicates some kind of *partial* interrelation: the individual economic processes are dynamically related to each other or with the general level of development. I do not believe that all countries of the world pass along the same road — but it is certain, and it can be supported with many calculations, that several important partial interrelations show characteristic dynamic regularities, valid for many countries.

(2) The main stream expresses a *stochastic* regularity. The regularity shown in fig. 1 does not assert itself equally in different countries; the relative weight of agriculture, quite obviously, depends not only on the general level of development but also on the na-

tural endowments of the country, on its external and internal political history, etc.

In this study no strictly defined statistical requirements will be laid down as regards the width of the band illustrating graphically the main stream. It will not be prescribed, e.g. what level of confidence should be used for establishing the interval representing the main stream. And it would be difficult to establish a general rule, since this always depends on the nature of interrelations among the indicators in question and their role in planning. In some cases even a relatively broad band can yield a useful footing for planning; in other cases, however, a much narrower band would be needed, and if the narrow band cannot be well fitted to the data, it would be better not rouse them.

I would not commit myself to any of the methodologies serving the quantification of the main stream*. Clarification of the complicated methodological problems is waiting for those specializing in international comparisons; I do not list myself among them. For the following discussion it is sufficient to assume that the regularities of a main stream have been clarified in some way or other.

---

* I would only mention a few examples in addition to the Jánossy method. Chenery (10) and in his wake a research group of the United Nations (69) tried to show dynamic regularities in the shifts of industrial structure with the aid of traditional multiple regression calculations. Similar research was done by the Research Group of Industrial Economics, Hungarian Academy of Sciences (see Z. Román (62), and the paper (67). I. Adelman and C.T. Morris carried out international comparisons with the aid of factor analysis (see (1) and (2)).

(3) There exist main streams the course of which seems to be independent of the *passing of historical time*; others, however get modified over time. An example of the first type is the consumption of proteins, which, though depending on the level of economic development, was the same for a given level in 1920 and 1970. Examples are provided of the latter type by shifts in the curves describing the interrelations between the consumption of consumers' durables and the general level of economic development. The phenomenon itself will be reverted to when treating personal consumption. It has only been mentioned here as an illustration of a fact of more general validity: the international main stream does not flow forever in its old bed, but digs out for itself, slowly but perceptible over a long period, a new bed.

(4) There are relatively few main streams that would be valid for all countries without exception. Mostly we have a *tendency acting on some major group of countries*. The scope of validity is delimited by various criteria (separately, or combined): similar socio-political relations, similar historical past, similar culture, similar geographical endowments, etc.

2.4. *Circumspect use*

The above qualifications indicate that the study of international 'main streams' should be used cautiously, circumspectly in planning.

This study has introduced two notions: those of 'harmony' and 'international main streams'. The two do not coincide. Among the youth of the richest countries hashish, marihuana and LSD are widespread. This is a 'main stream' phenomenon, but who would call it harmonic? Or another example: if the main stream of urban transport runs into traffic jams, why should we, too, be carried away by this stream until our transportation breaks down as in other big towns?

There are no secure, infallible footings available for planning harmonic development. Unfortunately, no *unequivocal* conclusions can be drawn from either the internal information outlined in section 2.2 or from the international main streams described in section 2.3. Many facts, uncertain in themselves, have to be used in parallel and confronted with each other, as well as with the sound reason and politico-moral conviction of the planners and economic decision makers.

The planner, investigating some particular interrelation, may start by studying an international main stream. Did Hungarian development proceed along this stream, from the aspect of the interrelation examined? If not, what investments and other measures can ensure that our development should coincide with the main stream?

But, if this was the first idea, it should be immediately followed by the second*: is it correct at all to be carried away by the main stream? Is there no weighty argument against proceeding outside it? And if so, do we possess the means to resist, or is the assertion of international regularity unavoidable? If a deviation is both desirable and possible, let us boldly deviate from the international main stream — but we should never do so without serious reason.

I must emphatically stress even this last half of a sentence. We should not dilute the notion of 'harmony' and equate it simply with the actual decisions of planners and economic politicians. A statement that: 'harmonic is everything deemed correct by the plan . . .' would be contrary to the spirit of what has been explained up to now. To hinder the spread of drugs is a deviation from the international main stream which makes growth more harmonic. But if a country spends much less on residential construction than is usual on the same development level, according to the main streams of housing, this is already a disharmony. We do not state (and this problem will be reverted to) that every country must proceed under all conditions and in every period on a harmonic path. *It*

---

* Order is of no particular importance. We may start from internal information and normative requirements too, and then, as a second step, confront them with international experience. The essential thing is to confront the internal and external information and to think seriously about their conflict.

may happen that disharmonic growth is historically justified. But the *qualification* should be distinct from that: we should by no means call disharmony harmony.

CHAPTER 3

REQUIREMENTS OF HARMONIC GROWTH

In the following I will list twelve requirements of harmonic growth. Before reviewing them, however, I have to make a few remarks on the contents of the requirements and on the way they have been formulated.

3.1. *Preliminary remarks*

(1) In my study I am going to examine the harmony of real processes, material-physical activities (production, turnover, consumption), and the closely related spiritual, intellectual processes. With the terminology of Marxian political economy: my subject is harmony among the *forces of production* and I will not analyse either the *relations of production* or their connection with the forces of production. As indicated already in

the Foreword, I do not treat how economic growth is related to political power and ownership relations, to the connection between the government and the population, to the class structure of society and so on. In fact, *even the institutional forms of the economy* in the narrower sense — using the term usual in Hungarian economic terminology: the economic mechanisms, the control systems — will be left outside the scope of investigation*.

Not as if I thought all these could be neglected. On the contrary, just because I believe that they are fundamentally important, I would like to refrain from a superficial and amateurish treatment. Even so, I feel my study is weak because it covers too much, and not because it pushed too many problems beyond the scope of examination.

This narrowing down will enable me to list such requirements that arise both in socialist, in developed capitalist and in developing countries as planning problems. Requirements such as that education and research must develop in harmony with production, can be justly raised either in Amsterdam or in Budapest, but also in Nairobi and New Delhi. Also the circumstances that gave birth to my study justify this delimitation: when a Hungarian planner is speaking to Dutch

---

* There are many marginal cases. Where do the non-material processes *immediately* coupled with material processes end, with which I have to deal, and where is the sphere which I need not examine, according to the viewpoints quoted? Unavoidably, the answer will be in many cases arbitrary.

economists, he is justified in putting the generally enforceable normative requirements into the foreground of attention.

It is a different problem that the actual formulation of the requirements will not be 'apolitical' since they have been formulated by the socialist political and moral conviction of the author.

(2) I have not aimed at *completeness.* Someone else might easily think that 15 or 20 requirements are justified instead of the 12 listed. If we dealt with economies essentially less developed than the Hungarian one, the list of the most important 10 or 15 requirements would be compiled presumably in a quite different manner. I made efforts, however, to keep in view moderately developed countries, similar to Hungary — and more developed, economically advanced ones. I stressed the requirements which may be characteristic of these groups of countries in two ways: either the results are particularly remarkable or the deficiencies and the failures in performance are particularly distressing.

(3) I can describe the requirements mostly in a *qualitative* form only. This indicates the immaturity of ideas; later research must lead to the quantitative formulation of more and more requirements.

Quantitative formulation is also rendered difficult because the individual harmony-requirements are usually not unequivocal; even in partial interrelations we may move within broad harmonic bands. It is not a single feasible harmonic path that is open to a country, but a whole set of harmonic paths. In addition, in the present state of our discipline, we do not even possess the tools to delimit exactly the frontiers of the harmonic set. We are capable rather of a selection; we may state about a path or a set of paths that it is certainly disharmonic. In other words: *we can mark out a set that does not contain surely disharmonic paths.* For the recognition of this latter set a survey of the twelve requirements of harmony provides some help, even if in a qualitative form only. However modest this knowledge may be, it is not trivial, since — as will be clear from a later part of the study — real economic growth proceeded for a long time, both in Hungary and in many other countries, along a disharmonic path.

(4) Harmony, as will be seen from the review of the requirements, does not mean a static soporific standstill, but movement, constant change. All requirements are of a *dynamic* nature. Their dynamic character may assume various forms. One form may be exemplified by the setting of a lower limit on the growth rate of some economic process. Another form by the definition of the relationship between the dynamics of two partial processes, e.g. the relation between the number of cars and development of the road network. Or, another, particularly important form: relation between some partial process (say, the telephone network) and the general development level of the economy.

Also these requirements must be dynamically interpreted, though — owing to the present rather rough, qualitative formulation — we cannot emphasize this explicitly.

3.2. Twelve requirements

I shall make efforts to formulate the requirements briefly, in a telegraphic form; only a few of them will be commented upon in detail.

Requirement no. 1: The raising of consumption*
In discussing requirement no. 1, the *average* consumption of the country's population, i.e. per capita total consumption, will be treated. The material composition of consumption and the distribution of income will be examined later, in the context of other requirements.

Requirement no. 1 can be broken down into partial requirements:

(1.1) The rise in consumption should be *regular and even*; there should be no slackening nor even a longer standstill.

(1.2) The rise in consumption should be 'tangible' for every considerable stratum of society. It can be

---

* For the formulation of requirements nos. 1-6, I have borrowed many ideas from the materials of the Manpower and Living Standard Committee for Long-term Planning. See the Report of the Committee (68), the article by Huszár, Hoch, Kovács and Timár (30), as well as the paper (29).

thus hardly less than an annual 1 or 2 per cent for any social layer or group.

(1.3) Relative changes in income distribution are unavoidable. Thus, if we intend to enforce the above principle (at least a 1-2 per cent increase to everybody), the average per capita consumption must grow faster than that. The lower limit guaranteeing that even the consumption of groups relatively lagging behind in the course of income re-stratifications should grow, is somewhere about 2-3 per cent p.a.

Our estimates are confirmed by international data. In countries where welfare is highest, per capita consumption has grown in the secular average by 2-3-4 per cent annually.

Requirement no. 2: Proportionate satisfaction of consumers' needs

After having dealt with the growth in the volume of *total* consumption in requirement no. 1, we will now pass to the composition, the internal proportions of consumption.

Our starting point will be the phenomenon of *complementarity*, in the broad sense of the term. Human needs are diversified and human nature requires that they should be all satisfied more or less evenly. This has been already mentioned in section 1.1, when clarifying the general notion of harmony; the idea is now only recalled.

Changes in consumers' needs can be examined as a function of several factors:

Income. This is a well known and, in general, a satisfactorily cleared up interrelation in the theory of consumer behaviour. Many interesting analyses have already been performed to determine the qualitative properties and numerical parameters of the fundamental Engel-curves. The phenomenon is, e.g., well known that with growing income the relative share of expenses on food diminishes and that of expenditure on consumers' durables increases, etc.

Social circumstances. Consumers' needs shift under the effect of such deep social changes as e.g. urbanization, the migration of rural population to towns; or the taking of jobs by housewives; or the reduction in hours of work and the concomitant growth in leisure. Though there have been sporadic investigations related to these social processes, we know much less about their effects on demand than about the influence of changes in income.

Technical progress. The Engel-curves, the demand functions shift with time, mainly under the effect of technical progress. In fig. 2 we present the number of cars as a function of the general development level and, simultaneously, of per capita income. The author of the figure (E. Ehrlich (17), (18)) determined two regression curves: one (the dotted line) fitted to the 1937 cross-section data of the international sample, the other (the continuous line) to the 1960 data. The curve shifted upwards between the two dates. Today every country claims more cars than were claimed by

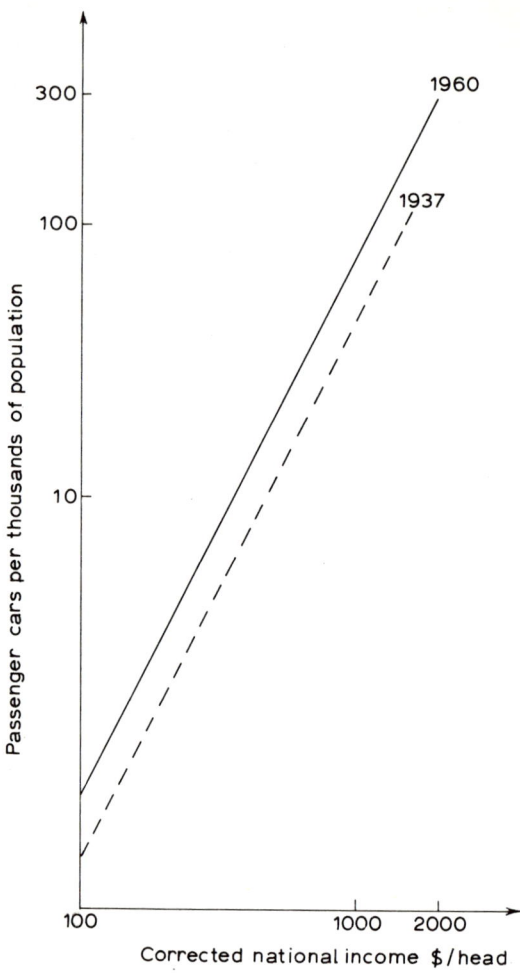

Fig. 2. Number of passenger cars as a function of the level of economic development.

a country which had been on the same development level a quarter of a century ago.

Even this simple example indicates that people do not have a preference ordering that would be valid once and for all: their relative needs change under the effect of many kinds of factors, mainly technical progress.

Inertia. Factors 1, 2 and 3 change, sometimes revolutionize the pattern of needs. Against them there stands another factor: inertia, custom, conservatism.

Relative prices. These are mentioned only in the fifth place, as an explanatory factor. Not that we denied their important role. Thus, they may e.g. accelerate or retard the suppression of old, obsolete products and services and the spread of new ones. They influence marginal shifts in outlays. In the final analysis, however, they do not affect the main proportions of consumers' demand determined by the fundamental complementarity relations among human needs. Maybe, smaller or major changes in the relative prices of clothing and food will lead to a situation where food expenditure will be 27 or 23 per cent instead of 25 per cent in 1985. But it will by no means be either 10 or 40 per cent. People may eat somewhat more or somewhat less, but they will not substitute a hat for butter or a suit for meat.

Here I should like to make a few remarks on the theory of consumption. Related to this, our remarks on complementarity and substitution in the field of consumption will be briefly summarized in table 1.

TABLE 1

The role of complementarity and substitution

Complementarity	Substitution
Develops the share, order of magnitude of the main groups of commodities (services)	(1) Influences the marginal shifts between the main groups of commodities (services) (2) Influences the proportions in the consumption of concrete, individual commodities and services within the main groups of commodities and services
Dominates the long-term trends of consumption, its 'main streams'	Influences the short-term proportions of consumption, the concrete situations within the 'main stream'
Planning (mainly long-term planning), must deliberately influence the 'strategy' of consumption, with a view to complementarity	The concrete substitutions among consumer goods and services, the 'tactics' of consumption, must be influenced by the market, the price mechanism

Undeniably, consumption theory has achieved many valuable results and the sophistication of its apparatus is impressive. Yet, in the course of working out the long-term plan, planners found that, indeed, they did not receive much help from consumption theory. Maybe, the theoreticians of consumption have devoted too much energy to analysing the interrelations between prices and volume and to fitting the theoretical construction of the demand functions into the axiomatic utility theory. But there is as yet little empirical material and theoretical generalization about the long-term historical 'main streams' of the consumption pattern, about their internationally valid tendencies. Theory gets entangled — to use the terminology of table 1 — in the 'tactical' problems of consumption, while the 'strategy', the study of fundamental complementarity phenomena gets lost*.

Speaking about the pattern of consumption, it is worth while mentioning another problem. Understandably, the ideas appearing among western intellectuals, students and politicians, about the modern 'consumer society', the overgrowth of material needs, about the attractive and repulsive features of the 'American way of life', have found an echo also in our country. Many people have asked the question: must socialist Hungary simply follow the main streams in which the consumption of developed capitalist countries proceeds? Or should we develop some particularly socialist pattern of consumption?

The finally crystallized answer, adopted also by the

---

* In 1961, the leading periodical of mathematical economics, Econometrica (28) published a summary survey of the state of consumption theory, written by one of the best known representatives of the discipline, Houthakker. We feel it to be characteristic that the thorough review does not mention a single scientific result in the field I have called in my study the 'strategy' of consumption, its long-term historical tendencies, and does not even list it among the important research tasks as yet not performed. (True, a paragraph of the study bears the title 'long-term dynamics', but discusses under this heading questions quite different from what my study calls long-term dynamics of consumption.)

author is not a simple 'yes', nor a simple 'no'. The substance of the answer is: we need not deviate from the main streams, if we have no special reason to do so, merely to seem original, for the sake of a 'special road' — because the majority of the population will anyway spontaneously claim the goods and services obtained by the population of more advanced countries, and that in proportions similar to those in countries on the same level of development as hers. For the most part, the main streams of the comsumption pattern express characteristic regularities in the development of human needs. If, e.g., synthetic fibres and plastics have won considerable ground in clothing, household goods and equipment all the world over, what should induce us to deviate from this trend of development?

However, this does not amount to following the economically more developed countries mechanically, without any considerations or criticism. If, e.g., in most capitalist countries books, theatre and opera-tickets are expensive and thus many people can afford them only rarely, we need not and must not follow the same bed of the stream and must establish other consumption proportions in this field, corresponding to the principles of socialist cultural policies.

Requirement no. 3:   Incentive and equitable distribution of income
The practical, numerical formulation of this requirement is always a far-reaching political problem. Con-

forming to his own political and economic conviction, the author wishes to ward off two extreme points of view.

One is to demand full equality. A certain degree of income inequality is not only unavoidable but socially useful and also equitable. It is necessary to compensate financially for burdensome working conditions, to acknowledge and stimulate special performance, to compensate for the costs and sacrificies of education and training.

The other extreme view is to accept without any criticism and even justify every income inequality. One may argue whether the viewpoints of compensation and stimulation justify a proportion of 1:5 or 1:10 or perhaps 1:20 between the lowest and the highest earnings. But there is certainly no kind of stimulation that would necessitate a proportion of 1:100 or 1:1000 between earnings, although such disparity between incomes can be found in several countries.

It is particularly harmful and wrong if whole social groups — because of their nationality, the colour of their skin, or their sex — get into a disadvantageous position in income distribution.

Requirement no. 4:   Security
In this context, several partial requirements may be established.

(4.1) *Full employment.* In general, the employment of every inhabitant capable and willing to work must be ensured. The labour reserve necessary for the flexible adaptation of the national economy must be maintained in an organized manner, in a way that this should not involve either material or moral losses for those in reserve. In the case where, owing to structural changes in the economy, labour is released, the subsistence and re-training of those temporarily unemployed must be secured.

(4.2) *Protection of health.* Care must be taken, in an organized framework — in the form of free or cheap, subsidised services — for the protection of the health of the whole population, for general social insurance.

(4.3) *Care of old people.* The main method on a moderate or higher level of economic development, is a general pension system.

(4.4) *Public security.* There must be strenuous efforts to liquidate the social bases of criminal behaviour, the population must be efficiently defended against those infringing upon the law, or jeopardizing the security of life and property.

In enforcing the above requirements total equality need not — and, obviously, cannot — be secured. Obviously a sick person or an old man who had earlier accumulated considerable means or whose relatives are well-to-do and lavishly care for him, will live under better material conditions than other sick and old people. The security requirements demand a definite *minimum level,* in harmony with the general economic development of the country, for everyone without exception, be he unemployed through no fault of his own, or sick or old.

Requirement no. 5: Opportunity for free unfolding of talents
Every member of society must be given an opportunity to develop his talents, in harmony with the interests of society. Every road should be open to him: origin or financial heritage should not mean either a privilege or a disadvantage that cannot be made up for; everybody should start from the same starting-line. In other words: society should be 'open'.

From among all requirements listed up to now, perhaps this is the one the meeting of which is principally a socio-political question. It is my conviction that one of the advantages of the socialist order of society is that it creates far-reaching *possibilities* for meeting this requirement. It rests, however, with the concrete socio-political mechanism and, last but not least, with the material conditions to what extent these possibilities will materialize. Conforming to the general character of my study, I will deal in this place with the economic conditions in greater detail.

(5.1) *Social contribution to the raising of children.* This requires society partly to compensate for keeping the family and bringing up the offspring (e.g. in the form of a family allowance) and partly to organize institutions for the care of children (nurseries, kindergartens, etc.).

(5.2) *Equal opportunities in education.* The fundamental tool is free education. This should be, however, complemented by securing auxiliary possibilities for young people with poorer cultural background than that of their companions.

(5.3) *Mobility.* This has many material conditions, from adult education, refresher and re-training courses to creating the possibility of changing flats if migration is involved. The society is only open if nobody feels himself chained for life to his first occupation and qualification level.

(5.4) *Social equality for women.* Here, again, many material conditions must be kept in view. Every trade, every job must be open for women. The burdens of keeping house and raising children must be eased — to this extent the task is related to requirement no. 5.1.

(5.5) *Increasing leisure time.* This is such a fundamental demand that it could be treated perhaps as an independent requirement and not as a part of no. 5. At any rate, it is certain that growing leisure time promotes the manysided unfolding of man's talents, among them also those which can not be displayed by most people in their regular jobs.

Though it has been emphasized in advance, as relating to every requirement, it must be stressed here separately that requirement no. 5 is of a *dynamic* character. The extent of its assertion depends on the general level of economic development.

Requirement no. 6: Development of education
The intellectual development of people, the enrich-

ment of culture, civilization and science are both ends and means of economic growth. This requirement is very diversified, only two partial requirements will be stressed here:

(6.1) *Fast development of education.* From studying the international main streams the conclusion may be drawn that the rate of expanding education is faster than the growth of material goods. Within total investments the relative share of investments into 'human capital' is growing.

While in requirement no. 6.1. the task of *extensively increasing education* is stressed, the requirement no. 6.2 now following will deal with *the internal pattern* of every educational activity.

(6.2) *Qualitative harmony between the demand of production for specialists and the stock of specialists.** The expansion of production and the transformation of its structure quickly increases the demand for specialists, beginning with managers, through engineers to skilled workers. Here too we have a proportionality, the assertion of which cannot be checked thoroughly with the aid of aggregated quantitative indices. Maybe every plant has a manager and a chief engineer — the problem is only whether they are

---

* Á.Kiss and J. Timár in their studies (35), (36) and (37) and F. Jánossy in (32), (33) and (34) are of the opinion that this is one of the key problems of harmonic growth.

According to the terminology introduced in the works quoted, there should be harmony between the job structure and the structure of qualifications.

qualified, talented and experienced executives. Maybe, if staff members alone are examined, the demand of the plant for skilled workers has been met, but it is unknown what proportion of them are old, experienced factory hands and how many among them have come but recently from the countryside and trained in haste, i.e. are but 'raw' skilled workers. The *qualitative* lag of manpower supply behind the demand induced by the quantitative growth of production leads to grave disharmony.

Requirement no. 7: Structural proportionality in non-competitive production
In requirements nos. 1-6 the 'human' aspect of economic growth has been pushed to the fore-front: the effect of growth on the living standards of people, on the enrichment of their consumption and culture. In the requirements now following, nos. 7-12, emphasis will be laid mainly on the 'physical' aspect of growth, on the problems of production, foreign trade and national wealth.

Let us start with production. I would not like to take a stand on the problem much debated now: to what extent should a country make preparations for self-sufficiency, for independence from international trade and to what extent specialize in the production of a few products in order to utilize comparative advantages. Not that I do not attribute extremely great importance to the problem of international division of labour. But it has many implications which are far from the main subject of my present study. Therefore, in formulating requirement no. 7, we have restricted our attention to the non-competitive sphere of production. A considerable proportion of production (in Hungary about 35 per cent) is in this category. The output of the following sectors can be completely, or at least in a considerable part, classified as belonging here: building materials industry, construction, material services (particularly repairs), some sub-branches of the food industry, transport, water and gas supply, communications, health, education. Let us call this sphere *non-competitive production.*

The sectors of non-competitive production must be developed so as to be capable of smoothly satisfying each other's demands as well as those of the domestic productive sectors competing with imports and the needs of final utilization. The requirement of harmonic proportions is here particularly important since a possible relative lagging behind cannot, even temporarily, be replaced by imports and thus causes lasting difficulties.

Requirement no. 8: Development of technology, product-quality and research
In requirement no. 7 we have dealt with the *quantitative* aspect of production, now the *quality* aspect will be treated. We have established three partial requirements and call readers' attention in advance to the fact that they are closely interrelated and partly even overlapping.

The first partial requirement is related to the combination of inputs, to the choice of technology. In formulating it we have neglected the origin of the input: whether it is a home-produced or imported raw material, equipment or machinery.

(8.1) *The up-to-dateness of production technologies.* Apart from justified exceptions, the technology, the combination of inputs, must be chosen so as to correspond to the international main streams of technical progress, and to the general economic development level of the country.

This requirement may be illustrated with the aid of two examples. There is a world-wide tendency for coal to be pushed into the background, and crude oil as well as natural gas are advancing in energy production. The second example may be taken from the field of transportation: the role of the railways is relatively diminishing and that of road transport (and of pipelines) is growing. The economy is developing harmoniously if, conforming to its own development level, it keeps pace with such world tendencies.

In this context I should like to make a few remarks on the production theory of the neoclassical school, in a similar manner as the neoclassical consumption theory has been criticized in connection with requirement no. 2.

The models, the framework of reasoning of the neoclassical school put the *substitution* among primary factors of production and, in general, among material inputs, into the foreground of interest. They are particularly engaged in the problem of how a profit maximizing decision-maker will find the optimum combination of inputs, weighing the relative prices of factors of production. Thus, the production theory can be smoothly fitted into the axiomatic utility theory, and into the monumental and aesthetic intellectual building of general equilibrium theory.

Far be it from me to deny the possibility of substitution among inputs or that price signals really exert an effect on those controlling production, save, that the actual role of these phenomena is much more modest and limited than that suggested by traditional production theory.

In the very short run, technology is more or less given. It is determined partly by the technical properties of the fixed capital, machinery and equipment, partly by the routine and self-repeating inclination of those in control of production. It is mainly for the *medium-term* that we imagine a possibility of choosing from among different technologies, combinations of inputs. *For the very long-term*, however, it becomes clear that, as a matter of fact, even the medium-term choices are deeply influenced by the general tendencies of technical progress, which break through in the final analysis.

The periodical changes in technology are reflected by price signals perhaps with great lags or in a distorted manner, depending on the concrete price system, taxation and customs duties of the country. The forecasts of future price developments are usually very uncertain. However important rational price proportions are in influencing decentralized decisions, in stimulating them into the expedient directions, it is not worth while relying exclusively on these. Part of the technological changes can be directly felt. We need not wait until the profitability of oil-heating exceeds that of coal heating — this change can be accommodated even without waiting for the long-term plans and preparations to be started (the production of adequate heating equipment or their import, the solution to the problem of transporting oil or natural gas, etc.). Well-founded technological prognoses have an important and active role in long-term planning.

Using the terminology introduced in connection with consumption: the neoclassical production theory got one-sidedly absorbed with the 'tactical' problems of input-combination. For long-term planning a theoretical foundation is needed that can be used in formulating the 'strategy' of technical development; which uses, with the aid of empirical-statistical analysis, the world-wide main streams of technical progress, the fundamental complementarity relations among inputs, the slow, gradual, but lasting shifts in relative input proportions*.

(8.2) *Improving quality*. Improvement in the quality of products and services should keep pace with the

---

* The researches carried on by J. Rimler about the 'joint movement' of various production factors, inputs and outputs, economic processes, about their complementary dynamics, are worth attention in this context. See (60) and (61).

growing volume of output. If contemporary transportation is compared with that of fifty years ago, the difference cannot be simply characterized by stating that today there are many more cars and aeroplanes. It is at least as important that the contemporary car and aeroplane is faster, more comfortable and easier to drive than that of yesterday. And the development of telecommunications can mostly be described as a qualitative transformation, and as the appearance of new products and services: we have today tape-recorders, television (even colour television), all of them also in transistorized portable form, together with stereophonic transmitters and receivers, direct automatic long-distance calls, etc.

Measurement of qualitative development is very difficult; it seems almost impossible to formulate indicators that would synthetically reflect the whole of the process. But the difficulties of measurement do not acquit us from the sin of neglecting this important aspect. Turning the pages in the huge theoretical literature on growth, we find that growth is everywhere described with extensive volume indicators, and the qualitative aspect of development gets almost entirely lost*.

---

* Let me quote here, similarly to the case of the consumption theory, a summary survey article, written by two distinguished experts of growth theories, Hahn and Matthews (21). The review, processing, as it does, a huge literature, does not mention a single scientific achievement that would have dealt with the qualitative aspect of growth; nor does it mention the research of the subject among tasks to be performed.

(8.3) *Promotion of research and development.* The development of production technologies, as well as the improvement in the quality of production or, using another term, both *process* and *product* innovation is promoted by research in natural and technical sciences. It is particularly development that is of great importance for every country. Research results may be perhaps taken over from abroad, but 'development' is a non-competitive activity that must be organized by every country itself. In this respect the international main stream is that amounts spent on research and development are growing faster than production.

Requirement no. 9: Balanced development of foreign trade and international financial relations
The restrictions mentioned when formulating requirement no. 7, are valid also for the treatment of foreign trade. We shall not get involved in discussing the problems of international division of labour. Renouncing any claim to completeness, only two partial requirements will be stressed:

(9.1) *Equilibrium of the balance of payments.* Very rigid rules cannot be set; the raising of loans, with proper conditions, may promote growth. It should only be stressed that a spontaneous and exaggerated growth of the deficit in the balance of payments is incompatible with harmonic growth. The incurring of debts leads to disharmony if the economic burden accompanying the credit is greater than the return of investments financed with the credit, and if the cover for the mature repayments cannot be smoothly created.

(9.2) *Qualitative harmony between exports and production.* This requirement is a logical sequel of what has been explained in connection with requirement no. 8.2. There it has been emphasized that quantitative growth and the qualitative development of production should take place in parallel, in harmony with each other. Now we must add: the export programme should be in harmony, in qualitative respects also, with the general level of economic development of the country, with the general level of its technical culture. It leads, e.g., to disharmony if a country, just emerging from deepest backwardness, immediately aims at exporting very complicated machinery, although it could not yet have reached a really competitive quality level.

Disharmony may be caused also by a mistake of opposite sign: if there are arrears in the preparation for an export pattern corresponding to a higher level of development and the country continues to export — in spite of general progress — the products of its traditional branches.

Requirement no. 10: Careful maintenance of reproducible physical capital

The meaning of this requirement can be best illustrated in a negative form. It will lead to disharmony if — while building with the one hand new plants, roads, flats, schools, and procuring new machinery — with the other hand we neglect the maintenance of old factories, roads, dwelling houses, schools, and old machinery. True, sooner or later the old buildings will be pulled down and the old machines will be scrapped. But they need careful maintenance up to that date.

Requirement no. 11: Protection of the environment, of nature

Productive natural resources, the treasures of the earth and productive land must be protected from untimely exploitation. We must defend the natural environment of human existence: the air, the water, the woods and the meadows.

Requirement no. 11 is today already an unceasingly repeated stereotype of every economist, sociologist, journalist and politician. But even if it has become a commonplace, it does not alter the fact that this must be considered a fundamental requirement of harmonic growth.

Requirement no. 12: Permanent keeping of reserves

In the wake of growth both production and consumption become more and more differentiated and complicated. Flexible adaptation to changes is increasingly difficult. If, therefore, we intend to avoid the shocks of adaptation, we have to keep considerable reserves in every field of the economy: capacity reserves, stocks of materials, spare parts and finished goods and labour reserves as well.

3.3. Polemics and delimitation

After having attempted in sections 2.1-3.2 to explain the notion of harmonic growth in a positive form, I would like to make now a few polemic remarks on other theories. To avoid misunderstandings, I feel it particularly important to delimit clearly my own ideas from other viewpoints which — though using perhaps similar terminology — differ in their contents from mine.

Optimal growth. The notion of 'optimum' as used in the neoclassical models, and the notion of 'harmony' as used in the present study, do not coincide.

The logical structure of the model of optimal growth is the following:

There exists a set of feasible growth paths. Though the authors have not always clarified this point unequivocally, they usually assume that this set is restricted by objective *technical-natural endowments.* Thus, every technically feasible growth path is an element of the set. The wishes, desires of society are expressed by the *social welfare function.* The existence of the function is a self-explanatory assumption of those constructing the model. The existence of the welfare function is equivalent to the statement that the planners (or those taking political decision) have complete preference ordering over the feasible, technically implementable set of growth paths.

For the sake of illustrating the problem in two

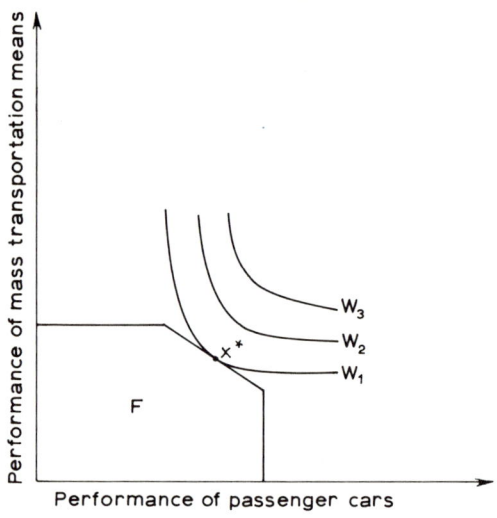

Fig. 3. The scheme of optimization.

dimensions, let us take a simple two-variable planning problem. What should be the proportion, in the terminal year of the long-term planning period, between the passengers carried by means of mass transportation (railways, ships, aeroplanes, buses, trams, underground trams) and those carried by cars (expressed e.g. in terms of passenger-kilometres)? The scheme of the traditional decision theory for the problem is shown in fig. 3. Set F is the technically feasible set of combinations of the two kinds of transportation means. The indifference curves W_1, W_2 ... describe the social welfare function (specified, of course, for this decision problem). The optimum program x^*, is

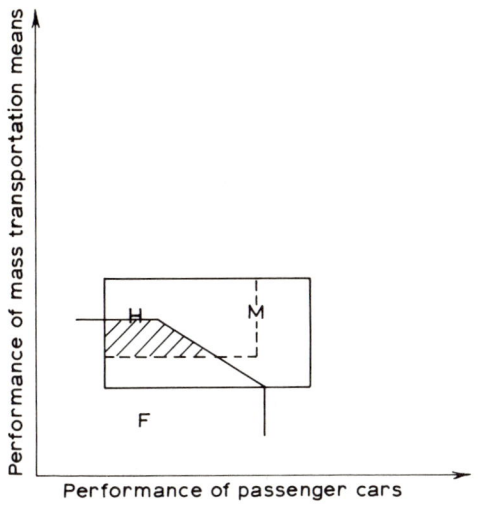

Fig. 4. Scheme of planning according to the principle of harmony.

the point where the indifference curve touches the frontier of set F.

According to the author's conviction, this is not a fortunate descriptive model of real planning processes*. The main weakness of the traditional model is that the planners or the decision-makers do not possess complete preference ordering; the welfare function does not exist. If we intend to build a true model for real planning and decision processes, another

---
* See some earlier works of the author on the subject: (39), (40) chapter 27, (42), (43) chapters 8 and 12, as well as the study (41). In comparison with my earlier studies I tried to take a step forward by trying to formulate a few normative requirements for the plans that can be accepted by planners and may be considered as harmonic.

scheme must be devised. The notions introduced in this study will be shown in fig. 4, related to the same problem as has been illustrated in fig. 3.

The rectangle M delimited by a continuous line is the pertinent part of the 'main stream'. The planners have arrived at an estimation about the average level of economic development of the country by the end of the plan period. The set M shows what combinations of mass transportation and cars belong to the planned general development level on the basis of international experience. Having studied the set M, the planners mark out a set H: this is considered by them as harmonic. Or, rather, we should formulate the statement more cautiously: they are convinced that the combinations not belonging to set H are disharmonic — while they are not quite confident that every element of H would be harmonic.

By the way, it should be noted: in constructing the figure, it has been assumed that H is a subset of M; it carves out the combinations assigning a greater role to means of mass transportation. It is from these that planners expect a diminishing of congestion in the urban road networks. But this is not necessarily so. With other planning problems it may happen that H has a part which is not common with M, and exceptionally it may even occur that the two sets have no intersection at all. This all follows from what has been said about the relation between 'harmony' and the 'main streams'.

But let us return to our example. In the course of

planning, the technically feasible set F will be partially explored. At least efforts are made to clear up what can be really implemented from set H, in consideration of keeping harmony with the other parts of the plan.

Finally, the plan target will be chosen from the intersection of sets F and H (the part cross-hatched in the figure), more or less at random, without a pedantic optimization process.

Even if we intended to work out not the *descriptive*, but the *normative* model of planning, I would not advise the use of the scheme in fig. 3 instead of that in fig. 4. Improvement of planning can be served by rendering the exploration of sets M and F much more thorough, founded more scientifically. In addition, planners and those taking the final decision should be encouraged to ponder as thoroughly as possible, their criteria of acceptance delimiting the set H*. But there is no need to 'compel' them to return to the calculation of a welfare function.

Balanced growth. The idea of 'harmonic growth', as interpreted by the study, is closely related to ideas on

---

* Important tools for this exploration, for the work aimed at analysing the effects of different variants of efficiency requirements and of moral-political criteria, at finding the limits to implementation, are the mathematical models. The programming models (that is, 'optimization' models from the *mathematical* viewpoint) are surely among them.

'balanced growth'*. I accept many statements of the adherents of 'balanced growth'. Yet I would indicate a deviation in respect of two problems.

(1) The school of 'balanced growth' is a loose grouping; the ideas of authors differ in many important questions. They are, e.g., not uniform in judging whether the parallel development of several (or even all) productive sectors should be listed among the requirements. Some are of the opinion that this must be absolutely required; narrow specialization is one symptom of imbalance.

As for myself, I do not support this concept of parallel development of all sectors which was widespread in Hungary in the early fifties. May I remind readers that in formulating requirement no. 7 (noncompetitive production) and requirement no. 9 (foreign trade), I stressed: I will not dwell on the much debated dilemma of 'specialization versus the broad-based development of domestic production'. Accordingly, I have not listed among the requirements of harmony the requirement of 'balanced growth' mentioned, the development of domestic production on a broad front**.

---

* The school has a long past. Among other authors, F. List (45), Young (66), Rosenstein-Rodan (63) and Nurkse (53), (54) can be listed here.

A concise summary of the school can be found in the introduction to an article by Streeten (64). (The article sharply criticizes this school, for that matter.)

** Though I do not treat this problem in my present study, I should like to indicate my standpoint, if only for the information of readers, with-

(2) The school of 'balanced growth' interprets the notion of equilibrium in the classical manner, that is, it requires the equilibrium between supply and demand. My own standpoint differs from that: I hold a certain excess supply over demand, admissible and even desirable. This idea will be explained in detail in a later chapter of this study.

'Turnpike-theorem'. The starting point of the theory is a classical study by Von Neumann (50), (51). This work by Von Neumann has an outstanding, pioneering role in the history of our discipline, and that in several ways: it is one of the first dynamic mathematical models; it is the first clear formulation of the duality theorem which later aroused such great attention; it is the first economic application of the fixed-point theorems worked out in the framework of set theory.

The problem is caused by the fact that, long after the publication of the study by Von Neumann, distinguished economists took too seriously what the ingenious work had to say in economic matters. The renaissance of the Von Neumann-model began with the book by Dorfman—Samuelson—Solow*.

(*continuation from page 56*)
out further discussion. (Otherwise, my view agrees with the opinion of many Hungarian economists and planners.)

In my opinion, a certain specialization in production, and organic joining in the international division of labour may be expressly advantageous for harmonic economic growth.
* See (13).

The authors have shown: if the economic system wants to get from a given initial state into some predetermined terminal state, and this transition takes considerable time, it is most expedient to take, as soon as possible the so-called Von Neumann path. On this path, every sector grows at the same rate, the input–output structure of production is invariable over time. Growth is fastest on this special path. This is like, using the simile of the authors, wanting to travel a long distance by car. If we can, we should avail ourselves of a high-speed motorway (a 'turnpike' in American usage) and should return to other, subordinate, slower roads if this is unavoidable to reach the final station.

The first turnpike-theorem has been successively followed by others*. In a few years a whole series of similar theorems have been born, which, though deviating from each other in the concrete assumptions of the model and in the mathematical proof, yet agreed in the economic basic idea.

Many economists consider the Von Neumann path as a special case of 'balanced growth'. I would like to argue with this idea.

In the preceding parts of this study I made efforts to highlight the fact that harmonic growth necessarily involves *shifts in structures.* This is testified by thou-

---

* See, among others, Radner (58), McKenzie (47) and (48), Cass (9) and Tsukui (65). Among Hungarian economists it was mainly A. Bródy who has been engaged on the Von Neumann models (see (7), (8)).

sands of examples when studying the main streams of world-wide development: we find continuous restratification, changes in proportions, in the relative weight of productive sectors, in technologies (and with that in the input-combinations), in the pattern of consumption (and thus in demand functions), in the quality and choice of products, in the qualitative properties of the labour force, etc. The *substance* of development gets lost in a theory which wishes to deem 'optimal' the constancy of structures, the equal rate of growth of all sectors, the invariability over time of input–output combinations.

Of course, simplifying assumptions are used in every model. This is justified if we neglect interrelations that are of secondary importance from the viewpoint of the investigation, or if we handle them inaccurately in order to be able to analyse the primary ones more clearly. In a *static* input–output model, for instance, it is permissible to use fixed input coefficients, if we use it for static problems (e.g. for drawing up an annual plan, or for planning the terminal year of a longer period). The situation is, however, different with a *dynamic* model, which intends to describe the path of growth over time. If such a model, by its assumptions, neglects in principle the changes in input-structures (e.g. the restratification of the input coefficients of the household sector, etc.), it has not applied a 'simplification' neglecting secondary interrelations, but has thrown the primary problem itself out of the window.

Further: I feel that the objective function of the Von Neumann model (and of the numerous turnpike models constructed in fair number later) is deficient from the economic point of view since, with unchanged inter-sectoral proportions, it prescribes maximization of the rate of growth. This is only good for providing a 'scientific' foundation for the growth rate fetish. Growth is not a rate-maximizing problem! The rate and the *harmony* of growth are equally important; neither of them can be subordinated to the other. If, however, we took seriously the conclusions that follow from the turnpike-theorems for practical economic policy, we would have to sacrifice the requirements of harmony, of flexible adaptation to changes, of structural changes, of qualitative developement — for the tasks of rush, for the maximization of the rate of growth.

CHAPTER 4

HOW TO MEASURE HARMONY

4.1. *A single indicator?*

The heated debate with the turnpike-theorem leads on to the subject of chapter 4: the measurement of the results of growth.

It is a widespread custom to characterize the development of some country with *a single* indicator; mostly with the average annual (compound) growth rate of Gross National Product, Gross Domestic Product or National Income. This is done by many politicians and journalists. And we cannot bypass their procedure by saying that 'they are not qualified economists' since the same is done by many academic people and professors in economics.

In chapter 3 I have listed twelve requirements, and some of them have several partial requirements in addition. Most of these cannot be measured with a single indicator even if taken separately. Let us think, e.g., of requirement no. 4.2 (protection of health) or of requirement no. 6.2 (harmony between the demand of the economy for specialists and the number of specialists available), or requirement no. 8.2 (qualitative development of products). To measure the fulfilment of any of them necessitates a whole series of indicators.

True, the analysis of the problem becomes thus incomparably more complicated. No use — we have to put up with this situation. No kind of effort at simplification can acquit us from the sin against scientific methodology and economic policy: of measuring with a single indicator. Medical science too is compelled to put up with this complexity when it describes the state of health of man not with a single indicator (e.g. only with his blood pressure or his weight) but, if it is necessary, it considers 10 or 50 or even a 100 indicators. Why whould we economists strive to simplify our tasks in an unpermissible manner?

4.2. *Indicators of 'flow' and 'stock'*

Whenever we study either the statements by politicians, or the abstract theoretical models of economists, they usually apply flow-type indicators (national income, GDP, GNP) for characterizing growth. As a matter of fact, stock-type indicators too are indispensable for describing the economic development level of a country*.

To measure national wealth is a very difficult problem. Yet it is not justified that the regular statistical observation of national wealth should be in such a neglected state as it is all the world over. Hungary is no exception to that. In spite of more than two decades of planned economy no comprehensive calculation has been made as yet on national wealth.

In this context, I should like to call attention to an important interrelation, which I will first illuminate with an analogy: with the example of *personal* income and wealth. Family A has been enjoying a high income for a long time, perhaps for several generations. Family B, however, has made good only recently. Let us assume that at the present moment the incomes of the two families are equal. A superficial glance might convey the idea that they live on the same level since they can afford from their incomes the same food, clothing, can buy a car of similar value and can keep it. If, however, we examine the *wealth* of the two families more closely, we will find great differences in favour of family A. They have more valuable furniture, paintings, carpets, jewels; perhaps they also possess a well-equipped holiday-home, etc.

---

* It was already some time after the data collection for this study had ended that the Central Statistical Office published its first calculations of the national wealth of Hungary. Their evaluation could no more be undertaken.

Family A had more time to accumulate greater personal wealth.

Passing now to the analysis of the relation between *national* income and wealth, I should like first to introduce a couple of new notions. Let us divide national wealth (more precisely: the reproducible physical wealth) into two parts: *productive* and *consumption capital*. In this division it will be neglected whose property the objects of wealth are (a person, an enterprise, a public body or the state), exclusively the *destination* of the object will be kept in view.

Consumption capital is every object of wealth that immediately participates in serving the consumer. So in this catagory is the household washing machine owned by the family, but also the washing equipment of the laundry enterprise. The following can be unequivocally listed as consumption capital:
— The wealth in households (apart from the tools of artisans, their stocks or the domestic animals used for productive purposes, etc.).
— Residential buildings.
— The fixed and working assets of trading enterprises and of material servicing branches supplying the consumer.
— The buildings, equipment and material stocks of the health service, education, and other non-productive servicing branches immediately supplying the population.

The fixed and working assets of all branches that do not get into contact with the consumers in any form may be unequivocally listed as productive capital.

There exists also an intermediary field: the wealth of branches which supply partly the consumers, partly the other productive branches. Here belong, e.g., energy production or transportation. With some arbitrariness, even the wealth of these can be divided between productive and consumption capital; e.g. in the proportion their outputs are used by the consumers and the productive branches.

Since the pair of concepts 'productive capital — consumption capital' has been first introduced in this study, naturally, we do not possess accurate figures on the proportion between the two. (Though I believe there is no obstacle to taking this classification into account when the Hungarian national wealth is assessed.) I have attempted, only to suggest the order of magnitude, to make an estimate, using USA data*. It turns out that of the reproducible physical wealth of the USA *more than half is certainly consumption capital.* This indicates well the huge importance of consumption capital in the accumulation of national wealth.

And now let us revert to the problem illustrated earlier with the example of the two families — but now in nation-wide dimensions. We compare countries A and B. The first has belonged, for a long time past to the advanced countries and grows relatively slowly. The development of the latter has accelerated

---

* As source of the data I used the report (71).

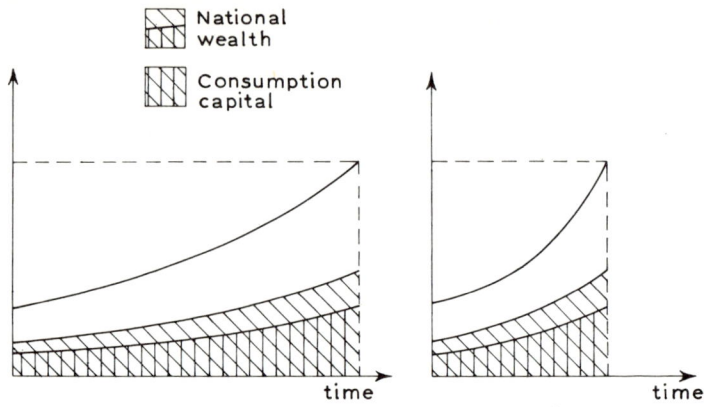

Figs. 5 and 6. Accumulation of national wealth and of consumption capital.

only recently; in terms of flow-type indicators, like national income, it has just reached country A. The typical case is, and this is shown in figs. 5-6, that although it has reached the former in terms of flows, it still lags behind in terms of consumption capital. In the short period of stormy development it could not accumulate as great a consumption wealth as country A during the long period of its more comfortable growth. Country B has concentrated its accumulation mainly on the expansion of productive capital ensuring a faster growth of the flow; and even within that on the less capital intensive industrial production, at the expense of the much more capital-intensive transportation. A relatively much smaller part was destined from total accumulation to the development of consumption capital (e.g. the housing stock, public utility projects, etc.), than by the other country. In our figures the diagonally-striped area below the (net) invertment function — its integral — gives the national wealth and within it the cross-striped area the consumption capital. As can be seen, although at the terminal points national income is identical for the two countries, the integrals of accumulation, particularly the consumption wealth in fig. 6, is greater in the case of country A.

From what has been said, an important practical conclusion follows for economists, planners and economic politicians in the moderately or less developed countries. We should not fall victim to the 'flow-illusion'! If we really wish to overtake more advanced countries, this must be secured not only in terms of flows, but also in that of stocks — and within that: in consumption capital.

4.3. Sacrifice — postponement — neglect

There is another problem related to that of 'flow and stock': the distribution of the burdens of growth over time. The problem is well known, its traditional formulation is as follows:

We may consume more today, sacrificing thus the future interests. Or: in the interest of the future we consume less today. The savings are used for productive investment. This accelerates the growth of national income and yields, in the final analysis, a greater consumption in the future.

Accordingly, the decision-maker has a preference ordering over the set of consumption flows materializing at different dates. The preference ordering can be represented by a utility function, summarizing the discounted values of consumptions materializing at different dates. The discount rate expresses the time preference of the decision-maker.

Since the study by Ramsey* the neoclassical, optimizing growth theories are based on the reasoning briefly outlined here.

In reality, however, the real dilemma of economic policy between the present and the future is somewhat different, and it presents itself at any rate in a more diversified form. It is not simply present consumption that must be confronted with present investment and, by implication, with future consumption. Economic politicians deciding on medium and long-term plans must take a stand in respect of the following problems:

Shall we rest satisfied with a relatively slower rate of growth in the near future, say in the next five years? Or do we want to attain a very fast rate whatever the means even in the near future? Should we choose the latter course, there are three intertemporal methods of acceleration, available to us: (1) sacrifice,

---

* See (59). In connection with the neoclassical growth models see the following comprehensive studies: Hahn–Matthews (21) and Koopmans (38).

(2) postponement, and (3) neglect. Let us look at these three methods in turn.

(1) *Sacrifice.* This is identical with one of the solutions of the dilemma as formulated in its traditonal form: less consumption in the present and more investment in its place. We renounce a present consumption flow and establish from the savings a productive stock. E.g. we eat less butter, export what has been saved and buy machinery with the receipts abroad, to be installed in a new plant.

In the case of sacrifice we renounce once and for all the meeting of a demand that does not accumulate; nor can its satisfaction be postponed. Let us assume that instead of an annual per capita fat consumption of 25 kilograms we consume for five years only 15 kilograms. After the fifth year we can again afford a richer supply of fat. Maybe, in the first weeks we shall consume somewhat more fat, but finally we shall return to a normal level. From that date we will not use for five years 35 kilograms of fat annually, merely in order to make up for the arrears of the preceding five years. We renounce once for all part of the fat ration forgone in the preceding five years.

(2) *Postponement.* In this case we renounce a stockformation due in the present (usually a formation of consumption capital). But we do not renounce once and for all, only the action has been postponed. The task of building consumption capital is accumulating, and the longer we postpone it, the greater will be the related burden in the future.

'Postponement' is mostly related to 'sacrifice' but conceptually they can be unequivocally delimited.

A characteristic example: the linking of suburban, rural or detached houses to the public utility networks: up-to-date water supply and drainage. Let us assume that we spend only half as much on these purposes as would be warranted on the present level of our economic development in the interest of harmonic growth. This, of course, requires a sacrifice on part of those now living in houses not yet joined to the water supply and drainage system. But beyond this, the task of creating public utilities does not lapse, it will not be deleted from the order of the day but, after all, we have shoved the problem off on the next generation.

As can be seen, as opposed to the 'pure' sacrifice described under par. (1), here we have cumulating needs that do not lapse.

(3) *Neglect.* We renounce present consumption (of a flow) or present formation of consumption capital (of stock-formation) in a way that this not only implies a burden for the future, but will cause express harm.

By reducing butter consumption today (sacrifice) we renounce something ourselves — and future generations will yet be safe and sound in this account*. If we postpone establishing public utilities in the villages, we

---

* Provided, of course, that we do not press provisions below the biologically necessary nutrition level.

have put a great burden on the future population. If, however, they are capable of making available sufficient tubes, fittings, machinery for civil engineering, and labour, for this purpose the public utilities can be created in the future without harm. It would do, however, irreparable harm if we sinfully neglected the training of teachers for some longer time. If we do not train a sufficient number of teachers for one or two decades (and particularly: if they are chosen from weaker human stock; or if their training takes place on an inferior level), the general cultural level of the country will suffer irreparable harm.

The notion of 'postponement' may be applied mainly to those processes in which *material* resources predominate. The rate of building public utilities depend mainly on how much of tubes, fitting, machinery and (relatively easily trainable) labour we afford. Since performance largely depend on the volume of material resources, a sudden *'leap-like'* performance of the task is conceivable. As opposed to this, the notion of 'neglect' arises mainly in connection with intellectual *'human'* processes — teachers' training was a characteristic example. There are no leaps in this field, nor can be any. Let us assume that the staff of teachers has grown for some longer time annually by one and a half per cent. It would be in vain to decide that the rate should be 5 per cent from now on, such a leap in acceleration is impossible. Education, research, improvement of quality, the training of leading executives in the actual process of

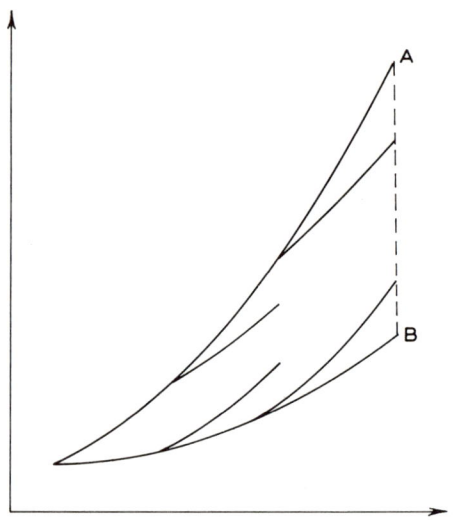

Fig. 7. Neglect — with irreparable losses.

management, all are examples for such 'organic growth processes', *for continuous development without leaps.*

The notion of neglect is illustrated in fig. 7. Before every decision we are standing at the starting point of an opening band. If we move again and again in the lower part of the band, after some longer time we will be separated by an unsurmountable distance from the path we could have been on by repeatedly choosing the upper part. We cannot jump, even with the greatest efforts, from point B to point A.

Explanation of the three notions, of the three 'intertemporal' methods for accelerating the growth

TABLE 2

The intertemporal methods of acceleration

Sacrifice	Postponement	Neglect
Renunciation of present consumption (of flow)	Renunciation of present consumption capital formation (of stock)	Renunciation of present consumption and consumer capital formation
The non-satisfied need does not accumulate	The non-satisfied need accumulates	The non-satisfied need accumulates
It is no burden on, nor damaging to the future	It is a burden on, but not damaging to the future	It is both a burden on and damaging to the future

rate, has been summed up in table 2.

Having separated the three notions on an abstract level, we must mention their interrelations. Namely, the elements of sacrifice, postponement and neglect frequently appear interlinked, simultaneously in the consequences of some concrete economic decision.

Not every sacrifice involves any postponement and neglect, but almost every postponement and neglect requires sacrifices, even when they are being committed.

Every postponement turns sooner or later into neglect if it gets unduly protracted. Perhaps it is burdened by elements of neglect from the very beginning, but this becomes obvious only if the trouble accumulates and presents itself in catastrophic forms.

Urban traffic is an example for the intertwining of the three forms. If the solution of long due tasks is put off for some longer time, this requires sacrifices throughout from the urban population. Finally, the transport system breaks down as is known from the history of several big towns. The effect multiplies, affects the whole life of the townspeople, their safety, the smoothness of productive work. Postponement has grown into neglect precisely because the trouble is no longer partial, but has caused a bottleneck for general development.

Though the three factors intertwine, their abstract separation in the minds of planners may be still useful. It is worth while to ponder before every decision to what extent the consequences of the decision involve sacrifice (which is admissible, if those interested are ready to take it), to what extent it is a postponement (which is, again, admissible, if it does not involve neglect and the resources released by the postponement can be used more expediently elsewhere). And, finally, to what extent some decision amounts to an irreversible, irreparable neglect or one to be retrieved only at the price of grave losses?

The problem also has ethical bearings: to what extent is the present generation under obligation to care for the interests of the future generation? But, in reality this involves a strictly *inter*generational problem only with a small portion of the population. The bulk of those participating in drafting the 1971-1985 fifteen-year plan are aged 30-50; but even younger ones do participate. Most of them will experience the effects of postponements and neglect *in their own lives*.

Far be it from me to underestimate the *ethical* requirements to be observed in long-term planning, but a considerable part of these problems leads to *efficiency* problems in a much narrower sense. To return to the former problem: neglect of urban transportation not only means that we have shrewdly shifted a grave burden onto the shoulders of 'future generations', but also that it will be much more expensive to eliminate the transportation breakdown than it would have been to forestall it. Similarly: the purifying of poisoned rivers, the new plantation of forests, parks, or orchards will involve much greater costs than if we refrained from the neglect which destroys nature.

In the final analysis, it can be established: *the growth rate of the near future can be increased not only at the expense of present consumption (sacrifice), but also at the expense of the future (postponement, neglect).*

This statement leads us back to the subject indicated in the title of the chapter: to the measurement of the results of growth. We have obtained a new argument against the practice which had been already criticized from other aspects: namely, of expressing the performance of an economic system comprehensively with the aid of national economic indicators of output with their growth rate. We should never forget to ask the question: what is behind the high growth rate? Maybe, it is explained — at least partly — by the fact that great sacrifices are demanded in the present and the future is burdened with postponed and neglected tasks.

4.4. The front-line of progress

I should like to contribute another idea to the measurement of harmony-requirements.

The capacity of a country, its economic potential at a given date can be described with suitably chosen stock indicators. This may characterize the size and composition of both the material and the 'intellectual' capital, in other words, the natural wealth of a country, its man-made material riches, its wealth and its most valuable resources: its stock of manpower.

Now let us establish *normatives* for the stock-indicators selected. Let us assume for a moment that we are capable of stating: what would be the absolute value of the individual indicators at a given date in the country in question if the different indicators were strictly in harmony with each other and with the general development level of the country. Let this be the *harmonic normative* of the stock indicators and let us consider the normative value of the indicator as 100 per cent. Now we can establish the actual value of each indicator as a percentage of the harmonic normative.

In figs. 8, 9 and 10 each indicator is represented by

Fig. 8. Completely even front-line.

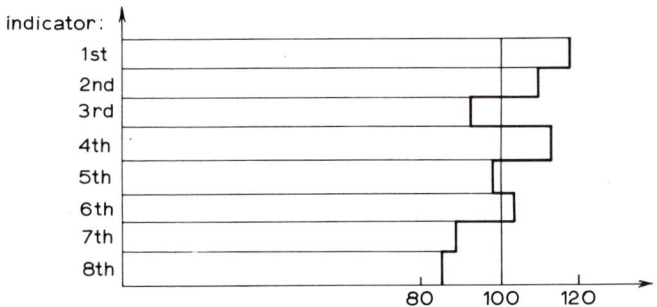

Fig. 9. Relatively even front-line.

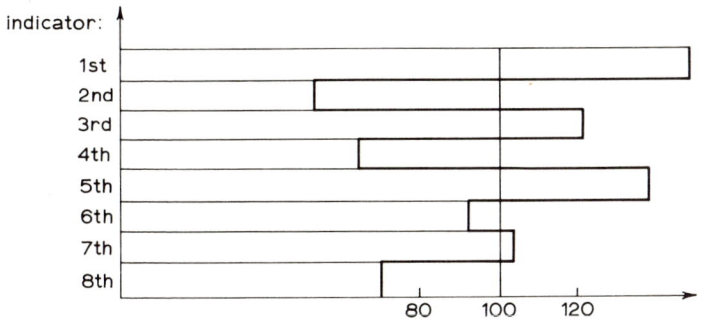

Fig. 10. Uneven front-line.

a horizontal band. I call the right-side limit of the bands put under each (the thick-drawn line) the *front-line of economic progress.*

Fig. 8 illustrates the ideal case: the value of each indicator is exactly 100 per cent; the frontline of progress is a vertical line. In reality this can never be realized, if only because the 100 per cent cannot be quite unequivocally interpreted. But even if we did know exactly the value of the harmonic norm, every real growth involves friction, a series of transitional partial leaps and lags.

We may rest completely satisfied if the front-line of progress shows the picture in fig. 9 instead of that in fig. 8. The front-line is relatively even, within not too broad a band. *The potential of the country is harmonic.* It is of course an arbitrary move where we have drawn the limits of the band: at ± 10 or ± 20 per cent — but it would be obviously wrong to allow a leap of ± 50 per cent.

As opposed to that, in fig. 10 we present a gravely uneven front-line of progress. Here the deviations reach far out of any band that could be qualified as harmonic. The left-hand inroads are the consequences of neglect for the stocks of the country. *The potential of the country is disharmonic.*

In figs. 8, 9, 10 we have presented three 'snapshots'. But a study of the dynamics of the front-line on 'moving pictures' is much more important. Also the terminology hints at this aspect: we want to describe not simply the pattern of the stock, its composition,

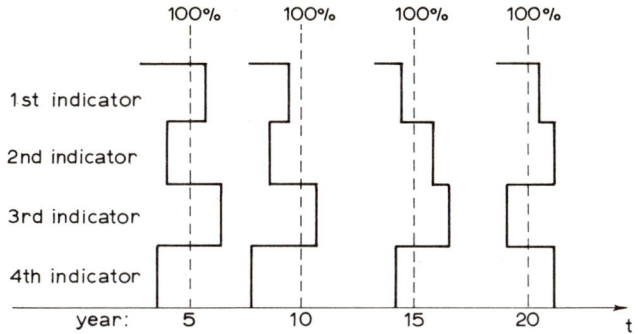

Fig. 11. Harmonic progress (moving front-line).

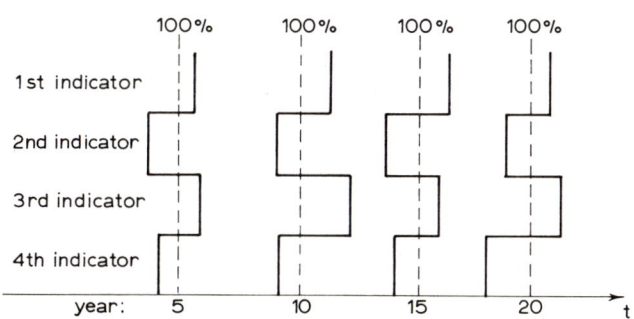

Fig. 12. Disharmonic progress (rigid front-line).

but the front-line of *progress*, that is, *a movement*.

Let us confront figs. 11 and 12. The horizontal axis has a double role in both. Partly time is measured with it: let us say, the stock planned in a twenty-year plan at the end of the fifth, tenth, fifteenth and twentieth years. On the other hand, with each year the dotted vertical line indicates the harmonic normative. For the sake of simplicity, only four stock-indicators have been observed. They could be, e.g., industrial productive stock of capital, the road network, the staff of those holding a diploma and the stock of flats. However, the figure does not show empirical figures, it only serves the purpose of illustration.

The progress shown in fig. 11 may be qualified as harmonic. The front-line, namely, changes its form: first one, then the other indicator lags behind or leaps forward. This is not only unavoidable, but sometimes even expressly desirable: resources are concentrated to carry out a definite task, wich may involve savings, economies of scale-relative advantages owing to large-scale activity. As opposed to that, the progress in fig. 12 is disharmonic. The inroads are stubborn, the front-line is rigid. Postponement becomes chronic and more and more turns into neglect.

It would be advisable to carry out analyses similar to those in figs. 9-12. It will do no harm if the establishment of normatives is uncertain, and we do not exactly know what 100 per cent is. The main thing is to follow, in a way similar to figs. 11-12, the *dynamics of progress*, backwards and forwards for about two decades each. Thus it will be more conspicuous whether we have to deal with flexible adaptation, with ever changing harmonic progress of the type in fig. 11 or with the case illustrated in fig. 12: with rigid disharmonies turned chronic.

And with this we have reached the subject of our next chapter: the analysis of disharmonic growth.

CHAPTER 5

A SPECIAL TYPE OF DISHARMONIC GROWTH: RUSH

5.1. *The factors of speed*

Having surveyed the notion of harmonic growth, its requirements and some problems of measurement, we may pass to the discussion of disharmonic growth. Prior to that, however, a few words are necessary about the factors in the speed of growth.

Above all, I should like to formulate a hypothesis – very cautiously, almost afraid of the multitude of dissenting opinions and criticisms wich I can expect.

I believe that, whenever a country has already left behind the first, stormy period of surmounting backwardness, the period of 'take-off', and is growing more or less harmonically afterwards, usually some 'normal rate' of growth develops. This is somewhere around

3-4 per cent (it may be 2 or 5, but certainly not 1 nor 7 per cent).

It is not impossible that the real growth rate of a country should be faster, even much faster than the 'normal rate'. But this always has some special explanation. There are no economic miracles. I will mention some realistic factors accelerating growth.*

(1) Particularly favourable *natural environment*. Here belong geological deposits, the climatic and soil endowments for agriculture, the existence of a seashore and the condition of a harbour, natural beauties attracting tourists, etc. It may be assumed — other things being equal — that Kuwait would grow faster than Egypt or the Sudan, being the richest country in the world in terms of per capita geological deposits. Kuwait is of course, an extreme example. Our neighbour, Rumania is much richer in natural endowments than Hungary; it has a seashore, and all that secures advantages for it in respect of the rate of growth.

(2) A particularly favourable situation as regards *international conflicts*. E.g. the countries that have not suffered destruction by war are in a favourable position. This can be stated about each of the countries at the head of economic progress: the USA, Canada, New Zealand, Sweden, Switzerland.

Here we mention, as a particular kind of historical

---

* For the sake of brevity, I will not treat the 'decelerators' which have an opposite effect. Part of them is simply the reverse of the accelerating factors: much less favourable natural environment, external exploitation, etc.

paradox, West-Germany and Japan. Though both were losers in World War II, it was particularly this circumstance that has led to their spending much less on armaments than the victors. The savings due to the abolition of militarism could be spent on economic growth.

(3) *External resources* may contribute to accelerating growth. This may assume many forms:
— Exploitation of colonies.
— Immigration. Particularly in recent times, highly qualified specialists, with valuable scientific and technical experts among them, migrate to the most advanced countries, while the costs of training are borne by the native country of the immigrants.
— Profits earned by capital operating abroad.
— Foreign aid.
— Earnings sent home by natives working abroad. (This is one of the external resources of Spain, Italy, Portugal, Greece.)

There exists no sufficiently thorough and objective survey about the real effect of external resources. Investigations of the problem have been as yet too much affected by various political prejudices, the viewpoints of propaganda and counter-propaganda.

(4) Development of a country may be accelerated by a higher *efficiency* in production and management than in other countries. Great thrift, full utilization of resources, full employment, particular zeal and consciousness of the workers, enterprising and initiative, quick introduction of innovations, prudent investment

decisions, clever foreign trade transactions, and so on — the phenomena belonging under the heading of 'efficiency' could be enumerated endlessly. We could hardly find a country where these exist all *combined*. It is, however, certain that a good many of the phenomena listed have played a role in the economic growth of the Soviet Union, Japan or the USA.

The active role of planning consists, last but not least, in providing for adequate measures to promote efficiency and accelerates growth precisely *with that*.

(5) Last but not least: the raising of the growth rate, measured with the aggregate indicators of volume, may be accelerated by the *intertemporal regroupings* mentioned in the preceding chapter: sacrifices, postponements and neglect.

Long-term planning is justified in providing for a higher than 'normal rate' of growth (say one of 6, 7 or 8 per cent) if it is sure that in the plan period some of the accelerating factors reviewed in pars. 1-4, or perhaps several of them combined, will be palpably active — or if it undertakes consciously intertemporal regroupings: sacrifices, postponements, neglect.

5.2. *Diversity of the disharmonic paths*

It would be a mistake to idealize any country. 'Harmonic growth' is an ideal construction; as a matter of fact, it nowhere prevails in its pure form. The real economic history of every country shows various deviations from pure harmony.

Indeed, everything that has been expounded in this study up to now is nothing but *a system of valuation* for judging different concrete historical growth processes. This is as if we gave the list of subjects taught in a school and its principles of awarding marks: on this basis the 'certificate' of each pupil can be established.

Let us have at least a glance at the development of the USA. Today it is the richest country in the world in terms of material goods. But its growth path was not at all harmonic — nor it is today.

Its affluence is partly due to the exceptional conditions listed in section 5.1: favourable natural endowments, favourable historical circumstances, external resources. To this was added (mixed with much waste) a great efficiency of production. And finally, we may find sacrifices, postponements and neglect also in that country. We wish to refer to the most characteristic infringements upon the twelve requirements introduced in section 3.2 only in headlines, according to the ordinal numbers applied there:

(1.1) Growth of consumption was not even; setbacks gravely affecting the population were frequent.
(2) Although results are tremendous in satisfying the material needs of consumers, there are gravely backward fields (urban mass transportation, the housing situation in the ghettos, etc.).

(3) Income inequalities are extremely sharp. There are great groups in a disadvantageous position, mainly the Negro population.
(4.1) There has often been mass unemployment (as at the moment).
(4.2) Although there are great achievements in health protection, general social insurance, the security provided by a free or very advantageous health service is missing.
(4.3) There is hardly any care for old people (and for a long time there was none).
(4.4) The bad state of public security is depressing.
(5.1) There is hardly any social contribution to the raising of children.
(5.2) Chances in education are not equal; the children of great groups of the population are in a gravely disadvantageous situation.
(5.4) Many kinds of material conditions for the social equality of women are missing.
(11) The natural environment has been gravely destroyed.

Many fundamental economic harmony-requirements are being duly met. It is particularly worth while stressing requirement no. 7: the proportionality of non-competitive production; requirement no. 8: fast technological development, improvement of quality, and the successes of research.

It is commonplace that the USA is a country of contradictions. Yet the above survey supports this truth turned into commonplace. The country richest in material goods is characterized by disharmonic growth.

The other countries could be similarly analysed, either the countries of post-war 'economic miracle', Japan, West-Germany, or the lately accelerating Spain: in each of them a characteristic ensemble of disharmonic features can be found. Perhaps, in the course of further research, the main *types of disharmonic growth will be classified*. For the moment, however, I dare not yet engage in establishing a typology. I should like to deal in detail only with a single type; in the following I will call it forced growth, or rush.

5.3. The 'pure' type of rush

In developing the notion of 'rush' I have mainly drawn on the experiences gained in the 1949-1953 period of the Hungarian economy. I will, however, make an attempt to go somewhat beyond the peculiarities of a relatively brief single period in a single country. I will interpret the notion of 'rush' — in the sense to be defined later — in a rather more general framework. A broader type of the disharmonic growth path will be given this term. Some characteristic criteria of rush appeared also in other socialist countries, and related phenomena can be found also in non-socialist countries, mainly in the backward, earlier colonial ones wich have now taken the road to independent development and wish to grow fast.

'Rush' is one of the 'ideal types' of the growth path (interpreting the latter term according to the terminology of Max Weber). It is a theoretical construction which has nowhere materialized in its pure form. We can only state that several countries have shown for some longer time phenomena corresponding to the symptoms of rush.

The practical measurement of temperature was solved by marking out two well defined temperatures: the freezing and boiling points of water. The scale between these two 'pure' points was divided into a hundred units. I would assign a similar role to the theoretical constructions of 'pure' harmonic growth and 'pure' rush. A considerable part of the real growth process is a mixture of the two (or of further 'pure' types not treated in this place). The construction of the 'pure' types facilitates the description, explanation and understanding of the mixtures.

Having justified the introduction of the notion, we may now pass to its definition. This will be given in a tabular form. The rows in table 3 are broken down according the twelve requirements of harmonic growth and the partial requirements related to them. The columns indicate the three intertemporal methods of acceleration: sacrifice, postponement and neglect. An empty entry in the table indicates that rush *does not violate* a requirement, while infringement upon some requirement is indicated by a cross. The

TABLE 3

Characteristic disharmonies of rush

No.	Requirement of harmony	Sacrifice	Postponement	Neglect
(1)	Raising of consumption	xx		
(2)	Proportionate satisfaction of consumers' needs	xx	xx	
(3)	Incentive and equitable distribution of income			
(4.1)	Full employment			
(4.2)	Protection of health		x	
(4.3)	Care for old people			
(4.4)	Public security			
(5.1)	Social contribution to the raising of children			
(5.2)	Equal opportunities in education			
(5.3)	Mobility			
(5.4)	Social equality of women			
(5.5)	Increasing leisure time	x		
(6.1)	Fast development of education		x	
(6.2)	Qualitative harmony between the demand of production for specialists and the supply of specialists		x	x
(7)	Structural proportionality in non-competitive production	x	x	
(8.1)	Up-to-dateness of production technologies			
(8.2)	Improvement of quality	xx	xx	x
(8.3)	Promotion of research and development			
(9.1)	Equilibrium of the balance of payments		x	
(9.2)	Qualitative harmony between exports and production		x	x
(10)	Careful maintenance of the reproducible physical capital	x	x	
(11)	Protection of environment, of nature		x	
(12)	Continuous care for reserves		xx	

'graveness' of the infringement is symbolized by the number of crosses.

Though every empty entry and all crosses in the table are essential for understanding the notion of rush, I would like to call particular attention to some major general characteristics.

Rush demands great sacrifices from those participating in it, from the present generations. But not only of them: it also puts burden on the future. It postpones investment tasks of consumption capital formation which are overdue. Thus, it may happen that the consumption capital of a country rushed forward on a forced growth path is much smaller than of a country turning out the same per capita volume but less in a rush.

In a rush quality is lagging behind quantity.

In a rushing economy there are not sufficient reserves: adaptation is not sufficiently flexible or quick. In several fields there are shortages in material, energy, spare parts, capacity, labour: the shortage situation frequently leads to strong tensions.

5.4. The causes and motives of rush

It would be an unhistoric approach to explain rush as the overambitious efforts of some statesmen. But it would be even more superficial to qualify rush simply as 'irrational' economic policy.

In the typical case, rush appears in poor, backward

countries. Such was the situation in the Soviet Union of the twenties; in several East-European and Asian socialist countries after World War II; but this is the background to the economic policies of rush in several non-socialist Asian and African countries. 'To catch up with the developed countries' is not only a slogan of megalomaniac politicians, it is the true wish of millions. It is difficult for a Hungarian, a Polish or an Indian metallurgical worker to put up with the idea that he must live worse than his American colleague because he happened to be born in Hungary, Poland or India and not in the United States. Among the inhabitants of the backward countries we may find people with various political convictions. There are those who think the political-economic structure of their countries is acceptable, together with the income distribution involved, and there are others who are of the opposite opinion. But everyone, without exception, finds it unjust that there should be an unbridgeable abyss between the living circumstances of two people performing the same work, with the same qualification, belonging to the same social stratum, merely because the one is the son of a rich nation and the other of a poor one. With diminishing distances, while tourism, the cinema, the television and the colourful magazines bring the way of life of the richer nations nearer to the population of the poorer countries, the tension is growing in our age. This tension, the knowledge of backwardness (and we should not be afraid to call it by its name), the very human feeling of envy — well, here are some important motives of rush.

This is accompanied by a feeling of danger, of menace. Such was the situation at the beginning of her fast growth in the Soviet Union; and it is certainly such now in China. The Soviet Union was afraid of being attacked, and history proved that her fears had been justified. Therefore, she made efforts to develop, as fast as possible, the branches which constitute the bases of defence potential: metallurgy, machine building, the chemical industry.

Though I have emphasized it in an earlier part of this study, I again want to underline it: the fact that rush is qualified as disharmony does not unconditionally involve *condemnation*. There may be historical circumstances requiring disharmony (or, making it at least understandable, explaining or excusing it). Nor is there a recipe of general validity to prescribe when disharmonic growth is justified and when not.

Accordingly, I do not wish to take a stand upon which country I would advise to continue the rush (or perhaps to start it), and which I would not. This problem could be approached only by concretely analysing the situation in the individual countries and it will be healthier if this is done everywhere by the native economists themselves. I for one, will restrict myself to the analysis of the Hungarian situation. Everything that will be expounded in the next chapter as a normative opinion or a recommendation, relates to Hungary, with no claim to generalization.

5.5. Harmony and the rate of growth

Having clarified the notion of rush, we are ready to return to the dilemma indicated in chapter 1, to the interrelation between harmony and the rate of growth.

Theoretically, there is no direct logical contradiction between these two requirements. E.g. a dynamic plan model is conceivable where the constraints prescribe all harmony requirements and the objective function is maximization of the requirements of harmony.

But, when drafting this study, I had in mind not the constraints and the objective function of an abstract planning model but the practical efforts dominating in everyday economic policy. And from this viewpoint the economic policy aiming at harmony can be clearly distinguished from a policy forcing the rate of growth even at the expense of violating the harmony requirements.

Since in practice no country can be found where either the one or the other path would have asserted themselves 'purely', the comparison will be carried out by means of a mental experiment. How would the growth rates deviate from each other in the same country if (otherwise under identical external conditions and starting from the same situation at an identical historical date)
— it proceeded along a 'pure' harmonic path, or
— along a 'pure' forced growth path (rush)?

On the 'pure' path of rush the aggregate indices of output volume would show a higher growth rate than on the 'pure' harmonic path.

The extent of the deviation would depend, to a certain degree, also on the indicator applied for measuring output. The closer we draw the limits of the output reflected by the index number, the greater the deviation in favour of the path of rush. Thus:

The accounting system excluding a part of the services (the MPS system) shows a greater deviation in favour of rush than the one including the services (the SNA system). This is only natural, since one of the criteria of rush is the neglect of services and this gets blurred in the former kind of accounting*.

The idea is illustrated in figs. 13 and 14. In fig. 13,

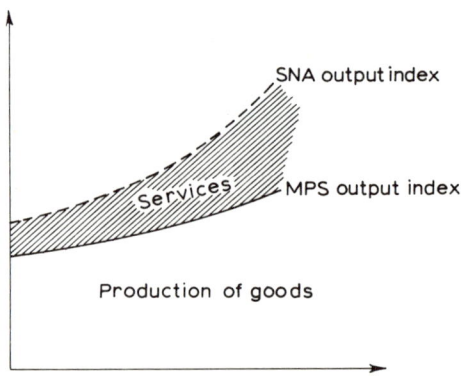

Fig. 13. Harmonic path measured with MPS and SNA indices.

---

* Hungarian statistics have shown for some time now the main data of social production parallel according to the two systems. Also the estimates of the long-term plan are being drawn up in both systems. When applying the SNA system, problems are caused by the measurement of the output of services.

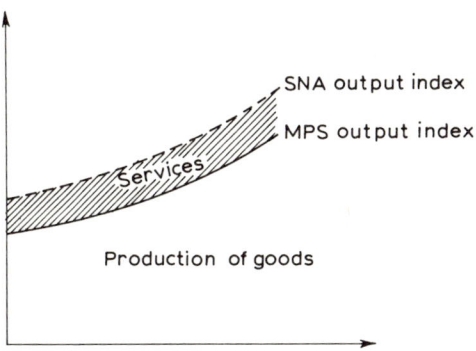

Fig. 14. Forced growth path measured with MPS and SNA indices.

on the harmonic path, the share of the service is growing, while in fig. 14, on the path of rush, this share is invariable over time. Now, if the two growth paths are compared according to the MPS index, that is, the lower continuous curves, rush seems to be much faster. If, however, we calculated according the SNA system and compared the two higher, dotted lines, the deviation would be smaller: the slower growth of production in fig. 13 is counterbalanced to some extent by a faster growth of the services*.

---

* Here I would like to mention a view frequently to be met but which is erroneous in my opinion. According to this one, it is, allegedly, of no major importance whether we calculate in MPS or SNA systems, since studying the real time series of the Hungarian economy, about the same growth rate is arrived at according to both indices.

But this is true only if we deal with a case described in fig. 14, that is, when the share of the services is more or less the same.

The debated opinion should be logically reversed. If, examining the growth of a moderately developed country for some longer period of several decades, we find that the SNA and the MPS indices show about the same growth rate, this indicates disharmony. In this case, namely, the harmonic growth of the services (that is, at a rate exceeding that of production) has not taken place in this country.

The deviation would be even greater in favour of rush, if not the whole of social production but only industrial production were examined. Rush — in comparison to industrial development — pushes into the background: transport, construction and trade and this is neglected if comparison is restricted to a narrower field.

Although the choice of the indicator has an important role, I would not like to restrict the problem to that. Let us choose for the comparison a comprehensive indicator of output, e.g. the index number of GDP according the SNA concept. I can only repeat the former statement: growth would be faster on the path of rush than on the harmonic growth path even if measured with this indicator.

This is explained by two — almost trivial — reasons: Firstly: in the framework of rush the share of consumption is relatively lower and that of investment higher in the national income than in the case of nonforced, harmonic growth. The additional investment deriving from this raises the growth rate even if, beyond a certain limit, the investment is implemented with diminishing (but still positive) marginal efficiency.

Secondly: in the course of rush investments are concentrated on those branches where the output/capital ratio is high (that is, mainly to industrial investments) and those where this indicator is low are lastingly disregarded and in a considerable part postponed. Here belong above all transport, residential construction, public utilities, trade and the services.

The explanation for the faster rate of growth in a rush can be given also in terms of the triple notion of 'sacrifice — postponement — neglect': sacrifices release resources in favour of productive targets, while through postponement and neglect investment can be centred to branches directly accelerating growth to the greatest extent.

But this cannot be continued for ever. There exists, of course, no rigid 'deadline'. It depends on political factors how much sacrifice the population is willing to make and how long. Historical experience seems to show that too great sacrifices cannot be expected for too long a period without graver political difficulties.

But it is not only the political effect of the sacrifices that may cause problems. The tasks postponed accumulate and sooner or later turn into neglect. And these may lead to economic frictions, losses, and even to serious shocks, e.g. to a shortage energy reverberating through the whole economy, or to lack of water upsetting the lives of whole towns, to transport breakdowns, etc. The worse the organization of production, the less efficient the production and the looser the work morale will be, the sooner will the forced rate lead to exhaustion.

In historically exceptional cases (though occurring) the forced high rate of growth slows down suddenly. It is, however, much more characteristic that the rate is slowing down gradually, perhaps against the intentions and rate-pushing efforts of economic policy.

When a car, rushing with high speed on the smooth highway, arrives at a hill, the bad driver may cherish the illusion that he has only to tread on the pedal and can keep his speed*. The result: the engine begins to 'cough' and soon gets throttled down. A good driver knows what to do: he must switch back to a slower speed. Then the engine will manage to climb the slope though slower but surely and without the danger of throttling down.

This 'switching back' will be the subject of the next chapter. While in chapter 5 we spoke about disharmony in *general terms*, now we will turn to a *more concrete* analysis of the Hungarian economy.

---

* The simile has been borrowed – with some modification – from F. Jánossy.

CHAPTER 6

HUNGARY IN TRANSITION FROM THE DISHARMONIC TO THE HARMONIC PATH

6.1. Meeting of the harmony requirements: the twelve requirements

The economic policy of rush prevailed in Hungary in its extreme, sharp form for a comparatively short time, four or five years. The leading political bodies, the party, the government and economists began to criticize the economic policy of earlier years already by 1953*. Since then the idea has been repeatedly confirmed that the rate of growth must not be forced

---

* Official terminology has employed several terms for the group of phenomena which I call 'rush': 'forced-rate industrialization', 'overtense plan', etc. A study by Jánossy (34) introduced another term: in those days, in his opinion, Hungary achieved, while striving at a high stage of development, only 'quasi-development'.

or chased; what we need are not overtense but sound, realistic plans.

In the past one and a half decades important steps have been taken in the direction of leading our country to the path of harmonic growth. Where are we now?

The restricted space available makes an exhaustive evaluation impossible. We must rest satisfied with a short glance at the present Hungarian economic situation. We shall take in turn the requirements of harmonic growth. I will stress mainly the characteristic features which deserve attention from the viewpoint of my study: harmony and disharmony.

(1) *The raising of consumption.* It is in this relation that the most essential change has taken place. At the time of rush material consumption had halted and even fell deeply back for a short time. In the recent fifteen years, however, the rise has been unbroken, there has occurred neither stagnation nor a setback.

In ten years, from 1960 to 1969, per capita material consumption has increased globally by 40 per cent, corresponding to a compound annual growth rate of 3.4 per cent*.

(2) *Proportionate satisfaction of consumers' needs.* Much effort has been made in the fifteen years to eliminate disproportions, but we cannot state even today that this requirement has been met.

---

* Source of the data is the publication (72) by the Central Statistical Office.

The improvement in *housing conditions* is slower than would be warranted by the general rise in the development level of our economy. We have lagged behind the level justified by the 'international main stream'. In order to get into the 'main stream' we would have to overtake in housing construction the countries on a similar development level as ours. Unfortunately, we can find several countries in the group of moderately developed ones in comparison to which our relative lag is not diminishing but growing. In this context, the five-year plan just started is promising since it essentially expands residential construction.

The lag is grave in respect of satisfying the *transportation* needs of consumers. But this will be treated later, in connection with requirement no. 7.

Similarly, the development of material and non-material *services* has not sufficiently accelerated. Let us think only of the backwardness of the network serving the repair of consumers' durables. This is, however, not a Hungarian speciality, but a disharmonic phenomenon appearing in several countries.

(3) *An incentive and equitable distribution of income.* Hungarian economists are not unified in judging the situation. It could be certainly improved, but there can be found no striking contradictions in the Hungarian income distribution that would sharply affect broader strata.

(4.1) *Full employment.* This has been secured throughout (in the period of rush and ever since); this is a major achievement of our system.

(4.2) *Protection of health.* We can register many achievements, mainly that social insurance is practically general, together with a free or reduced-rate hospital treatment for the population. There are, however, disproportions. Only two cases will be mentioned. In respect of the number of doctors per head of population Hungary occupies the distinguished 9th place in Europe. But in comparison to that we are lagging behind as regards the number of hospital beds per head of population: in this list Hungary occupies only the 17th place. One of the fields where 'postponement' prevails is the construction of hospitals*.

(4.3) *Pensions.* We have a general pension system. True, the level of pensions is modest. But the fact itself, the state organization for the care for old people, can be considered as an important achievement.

(4.4) *Public security.* We have no special reason for complaint. Public security is essentially better than in many richer countries.

About the requirements 4.1-4.4 it may be comprehensively stated: our results in respect of the *safety* of material and social living circumstances are considerable. This is a factor frequently neglected in international comparisons which focus attention exclusively on one or two indicators of volume (e.g. per capita consumption, etc.).

---

* Source of the data is the publication (25) of the Manpower and Living Standard Committee for Long-term Planning.

(5) *Possibility for a free unfolding of talents.* It would be difficult to award here a comprehensive 'mark'. In satisfying these requirements great achievements and deplorable neglect are mixed. I restrict myself to stressing the most important result: free education. This is the most important material basis allowing our youth to start from a common line. This is complemented by many other measures. Yet we cannot state that chances are really equal and that a career is equally open to everyone. There can be no doubt that the young people who have been educated in less cultured homes, whose parents could provide less financial help for extra lessons, learning languages, buying books and who have fewer personal acquaintances for smoothing the way of the young, etc., still start with a handicap. But this leads to a range of problems that would grow beyond the scope of my study — I wanted rather to signal the existence of the problem.

(6.1) *Fast development of education.* The situation is characterized by considerable development on the one hand and by many kinds of postponement and neglect on the other. Thus, e.g., the lower salary level of the teaching personnel was a neglect that will, I am afraid, produce its disadvantageous effects for a long time in the not sufficiently demanding selection of personnel and, in the final analysis, in the quality of education. In addition, there is a lag in respect of educational investments, in the renewal and development of buildings and equipment. On the economic development level corresponding to Hungary's present situation about 4.5-5 per cent of GDP is spent on education, but Hungary has spent less*.

(6.2) *Qualitative harmony between the demand of production for qualified people and the stock of qualified personnel.* The fast flow from the countryside to the towns is subsiding. Production begins to digest the 'raw' labour who have come into the factories in recent decades: they are now becoming real industrial workers. In this respect we seem to have advanced towards harmony.

(7) *Structural proportionality in non-competitive production.* Similarly to the earlier parts of this study, we will not deal here with the part of production competing with imports. The question is most closely interrelated with the problems of international division of labour, specialization and self-sufficiency, and these I have excluded from the scope of my study. Therefore, I would make remarks only in connection with a single branch, and this is *transport and communication.* No doubt, this belongs in its majority to the category of non-competitive production. We may import cars or aeroplanes, but the road, the petrol station, the repair shop, the tracks, the port of the airport must be here, in Hungary.

Beside residential construction, this is the field where the phenomenon I call 'postponement' mainly appears. All over the world, including Hungary, many

---

* Sources: book (44) by J. Kovács and paper (11).

opinions emerged about motoring. There are people who are glad of its spreading while others are angry about it and consider it one of the most harmful tendencies of our age. The process can be slowed down to a certain extent*, provided that transport demands are satisfied in some other way. But, sooner or later, the tendency breaks through. With rising living standards also the number of cars increases. The horse-drawn cart has been already replaced by the truck and in the competition between the railways and trucks the former have essential disadvantages from several points of view, so that the share of the latter is bound to increase.

In Hungary the number of cars is rapidly growing, though we are lagging behind in comparison to the

---

* The following story was told in the Hungarian Planning Office with some self-mockery:

At a conference the long-term plan for motoring was discussed and several people fought against the rapid raising of the number of cars, with well supported arguments: they pollute the air, cause congestion in the big towns, etc. When, however, the participants had a closer look at each other, they discovered that each of them, both advocates of and opposers to motorism had their own cars.

international 'main stream'. This is shown in fig. 15*. In reality, however, the gravest problem is not this one. As a matter of fact, it is easy to increase the number of cars, even suddenly. If domestic production lags it is only a problem of foreign exchange. The real problem is caused by *the goods complementing motorism.* This is where there is already a shortage today, with the present stock of cars. In this category are the repair network and the stocks of spare parts, the network of petrol stations, the traffic lamps and signs, and principally: the roads. Road building engages huge material resources. This is a task that was pushed to the background in our country for years – and the neglect continues. We spend much less on roads than the countries which we ought to catch up with by means of an accelerated road-building pro-

---

* The basis of figs. 15 and 16 is formed from corresponding figures in the article (26) by the West-German economist Hoffmann. Hoffmann made calculations using the data of 21 capitalist countries for years around 1966. In the case of fig. 15, Hoffmann's figure has been taken over without any change, together with the regression line calculated by him and then I noted in the figure Hungary's place in 1966. In the case of fig. 16, the points in Hoffmann's figure have been taken over, to these I calculated a regression line and noted Hungary's place in 1966.

I must confess that, by using the two figures, I have come into conflict, to some extent, with the earlier reasoning of my study. Hoffmann considered here, namely, the standard GNP data as measures of development, although I have explained why this may give a somewhat one-sided picture. I hope, however, that this inconsistency will not lead to misunderstandings. For lack of a better indicator the two figures may give a picture about the relative backwardness of this important sphere in their present form.

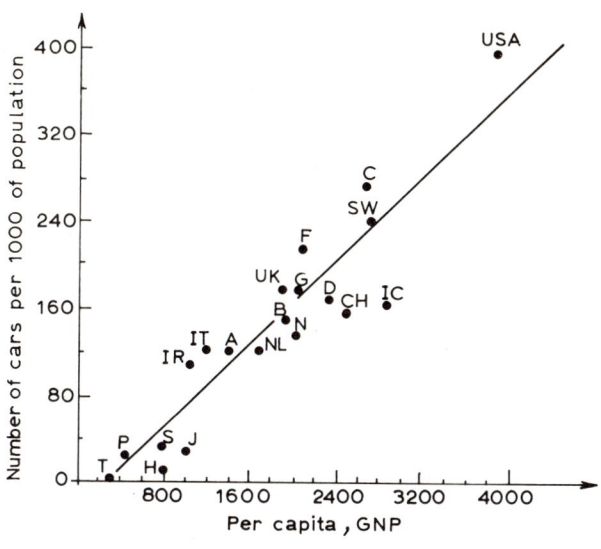

A	– Austria	NL	– Netherlands
B	– Belgium	N	– Norway
C	– Canada	P	– Portugal
D	– Denmark	S	– Spain
F	– France	SW	– Sweden
G	– Fed. Rep. of Germany	CH	– Switzerland
IC	– Iceland	T	– Turkey
IR	– Ireland	UK	– United Kingdom
IT	– Italy	USA	– United States
J	– Japan	H	– Hungary

Fig. 15. The 'main stream' for the number of cars.

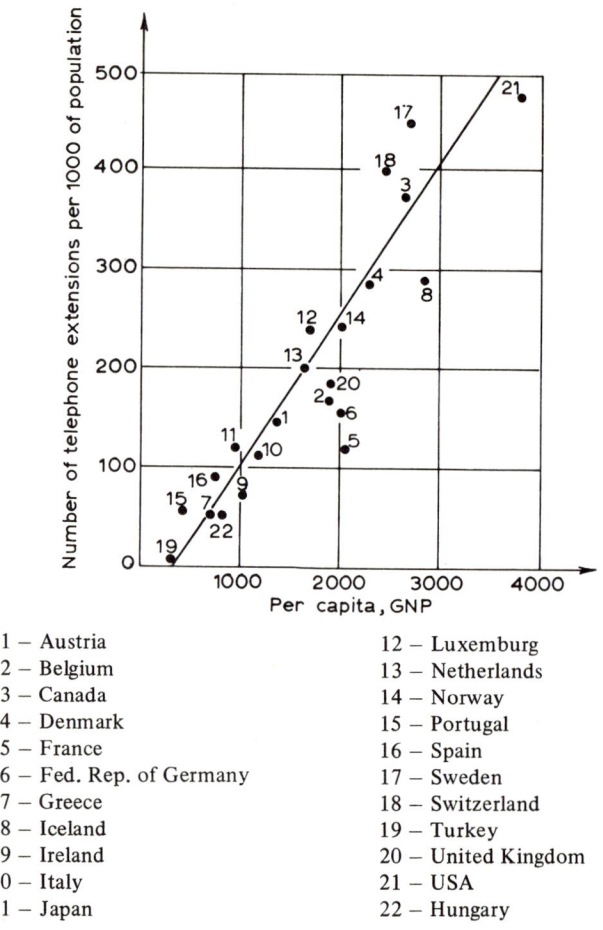

1 – Austria
2 – Belgium
3 – Canada
4 – Denmark
5 – France
6 – Fed. Rep. of Germany
7 – Greece
8 – Iceland
9 – Ireland
10 – Italy
11 – Japan
12 – Luxemburg
13 – Netherlands
14 – Norway
15 – Portugal
16 – Spain
17 – Sweden
18 – Switzerland
19 – Turkey
20 – United Kingdom
21 – USA
22 – Hungary

Fig. 16. The 'main stream' for the number of telephone extensions.

gramme. Thus e.g. Switzerland spends on the building and maintenance of roads 2.7 per cent of its GDP, West-Germany 2.6 per cent, Finland 2.2 per cent, while Hungary only 0.9 per cent*.

The means of urban mass transportation are overcrowded all over the world, it is thus not worth while contrasting our situation with the 'main stream'. It must be told, however, that we have lagged behind the demand of the population in several fields. We cannot comfort ourselves that the slower growth in the number of cars has been compensated for by a quicker development of mass transportation.

In communications the picture is not uniform. Thus, e.g., we have succeeded in overtaking the 'main stream' in spreading television. But there is a serious lag in developing the telephone network, as clearly indicated by fig. 16.

(8.1) *The up-to-dateness of production technologies.* Certainly deficiencies may be found in meeting this requirement, but this is not one of the characteristic problems of our economy. In this respect we could keep pace in most fields of production with the general development level of our growth.

(8.2) *Improvement of quality.* This is, indeed, one of our gravest problems. Though the quality of many of our products has improved, there are many justified complaints. One of the most persistent remnants of

---
* Source of the data (70).

the era of rush is the lagging of quality behind the quantitative growth of production.

(8.3) *Promotion of research and development.* The situation is similar to that relating to requirement no. 8.1: though there may be partial disproportions, in general we are not lagging behind in supporting research. The fact that quality is not improving satisfactorily is not due to possible neglect in research but can be explained mainly by the chronic equilibrium disturbances of the market and by deficiencies in the system of economic control and incentives (see chapters 7 and 8).

(9.1) *Equilibrium of the balance of payments.* The quantitative and qualitative development of exports is uneven; upswings are followed by slumps. We have not succeeded in overcoming our foreign trade difficulties permanently. Here also we have to face the problem of 'postponement': though it has been repeatedly decided to settle matters *now*, the settling of foreign trade problems is in the end put off until next year.

(9.2) *Qualitative harmony between exports and production.* In this context I would refer to an analysis investigating the situation of Hungarian machinery exports*. One of the major results of the analysis is presented in fig. 17. The horizontal axis shows, as an indicator of the general economic development level,

---

* The research was done by Z. Bekker, her results were summed up in the article (5). The statements of the analysis and the figure itself have been taken from her article.

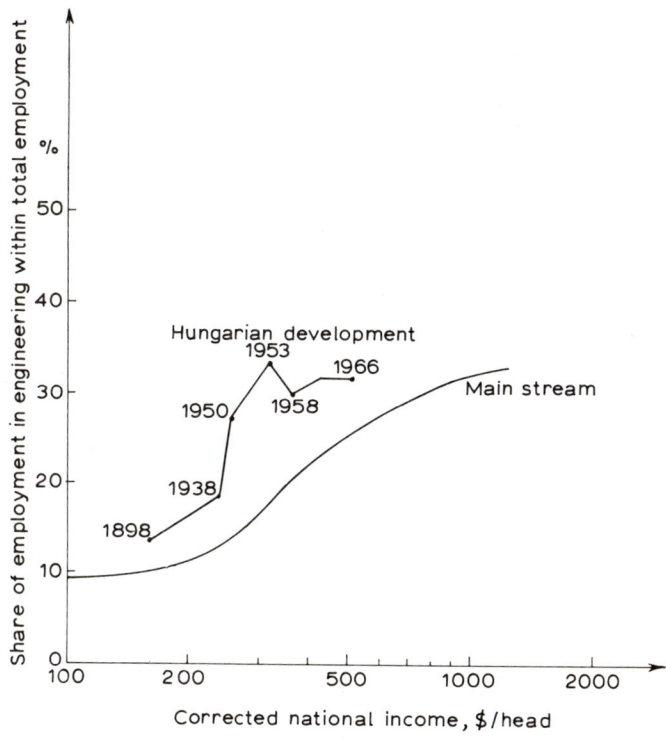

Fig. 17. Development of the engineering (metal working) industries.

the corrected national income per capita, the vertical one (to indicate the share of engineering industries) employment in the engineering branches as a percentage of total industrial employment. The lower curve in the figure is the international 'main stream'. The upper curve is the line of Hungarian development.

The figure shows that Hungary advanced, both at the start and at the end of the period observed, somewhat above the main stream*. However, at the time of sharply enforced rush the line jumped with a great bend high above the main stream. Later, however, we approached closer and closer to the main stream.

The development of engineering is correct and one of the phenomena accompanying the general growth of the economy. It is also understandable that we do not produce every machine at home but specialize to a certain extent: we have machinery exports and imports. It does not seem, however, justified that Hungary should specialize in producing machinery to a greater extent than, let us say, West-Germany, or Switzerland — there are no efficiency or moral or political arguments in support of it.

A different picture is obtained if *not* machinery *production*, but merely machinery *exports* into developed countries are examined. In this latter respect the Hungarian data closely follow the curve of the international main stream; we do not export either more or less machinery to the developed countries than others on a similar development level. This can be explained by the fact that increasing the *volume* of output is more or less a matter of decision. If we create more machinery factories, production will be greater. The

---

* The study by Bekker describes the main stream with a single curve, not a band. If it were represented by a band along the curve, it would perhaps turn out that the beginning and the end of the Hungarian path fall into the band or are not far from it.

success of exports to the developed countries, however, depends mainly on the *quality* of the Hungarian machines. But, as I have emphasized earlier, the improvement of quality is an 'organic process'. It cannot be suddenly improved by mere decision: for this technical education, routine, competence must be assiduously and patiently improved.

In the case of engineering fig. 17 shows that exports and the quality pattern of production are gradually coming into harmony. This is true also for other industries and may be regarded as a general tendency. From this point of view we have substantially approached the meeting of the harmony requirement.

(10) *Careful maintenance of the reproducible physical capital.* It is difficult to put together a comprehensive picture. It seems, however, that the maintenance of existing older residential and public buildings and roads and in several industries the maintenance of old machinery and means of transportation as well is still lagging behind, while rapidly establishing new projects.

(11) *Protection of nature.* We have reached a level of economic development where the destruction of the natural environment becomes a real danger. We have as yet made few mistakes and have, perhaps, not yet caused final, irreparable harm but, unfortunately, we cannot state either that every necessary precaution has been taken to protect nature. Only a single example will be mentioned: although we are still on a moderate level in both industrial development and in

motoring, Budapest already is at the 'head' on a world scale as regards air pollution. The protection of nature requires substantial resources in the future.

(12) *Constant care for reserves.* Though shortages have been eased in several fields — in comparison to the peak of rush — they are still widely felt. Supply often lags behind demand both as regards the consumer market and in the productive sphere, but particularly in the investment goods market. This phenomenon will be dealt with separately in chapter 8.

6.2. Satisfying the requirements of harmony: summing up

Having looked in turn at the twelve requirements of harmony, how they are being met in Hungary, we will now sum up our statements, with the aid of table 4. Its structure is identical with that of table 3, which was used to define the 'pure' type of rush. In fig. 4 crosses can be found only where one or the other requirement of harmony is still being infringed upon now, in the seventies. By contrasting the two tables it can be established (if only in a highly aggregated and simplified form) in what respect we are still following and in what we have deviated from the path of 'rush'.

The most important change in comparison to the period 1949-1953 appears in satisfying requirement no. 1: *consumption is regularly and considerably*

TABLE 4

Present satisfaction of the harmony requirements

No.	Requirement of harmony	Sac-rifice	Post-ponement	Neglect
(1)	Raising of consumption			
(2)	Proportionate satisfaction of consumers' needs	XX	XX	
(3)	Incentive and equitable distribution of income			
(4.1)	Full employment			
(4.2)	Protection of health		X	
(4.3)	Care for old people			
(4.4)	Public security			
(5.1)	Social contribution to the raising of children			
(5.2)	Equal opportunities in education			
(5.3)	Mobility			
(5.4)	Social equality of women			
(5.5)	Increasing leisure time	X		
(6.1)	Fast development of education		X	
(6.2)	Qualitative harmony between the demand of production for specialists and the supply of specialists			
(7)	Structural proportionality in non-competitive production	X	XX	
(8.1)	Up-to-dateness of production technologies			
(8.2)	Improvement of quality	X	X	X
(8.3)	Promotion of research and development			
(9.1)	Equilibrium of the balance of payments		X	
(9.2)	Qualitative harmony between exports and production			
(10)	Careful maintenance of the reproducible physical capital	X	X	
(11)	Protection of environment, of nature		X	X
(12)	Continuous care for reserves		X	

growing. This is of fundamental importance. This single change would suffice to ensure that the economic development of the last one and a half decades should not be judged as 'rush' in the classical sense.

At the same time, it cannot be unequivocally stated that we have shifted to a harmonic growth path. Closely comparing tables 3 and 4, we may establish that quite a few requirements are not met even today; perhaps we find only one cross in some entries instead of two, but we find some where the situation corresponds to the typical symptoms of 'rush' even today.

For one and a half decades Hungary has been in a state of transition between rush and the harmonic growth path. This shift is, however, slow, in many details it is inconsistent and even relapsing; many kinds of old postponements and neglect continue. The transition is not really planned; it is full of improvisation, of measures taken under the pressure of old evils.

To these comments it may be added that the transition was made timidly and awkwardly.

Here we must again revert to the dilemma with which I started my study: the conflict between the 'harmony-soul' and the 'growth-rate soul'. At the end of the preceding chapter this was mentioned *in general terms,* in the context of comparing, in an abstract manner, the 'pure' harmonic and the 'pure' forced paths. Now, however, it is the *concrete* analysis of the present Hungarian situation that requires us to raise the problem again.

There are as yet no final decisions on the fifteen-year plan. The materials drawn up and the discussions which have taken place up to now reflect this conflict. The desire for harmony is expressed in a hundred forms. But it seems as if we shied away from facing the fact that this may probably lead to a reduction in the growth rate of the aggregate indices of volume; as if we were ashamed to lag behind the growth rate of one or the other country. As a matter of fact, there is nothing to be ashamed of. Neither the present nor the future generation and much less history will evaluate the present economic policy of our country by the growth rate achieved, but much more by whether we succeed in setting in order, in consolidating the economy of Hungary and in making people more contented.

6.3. *Transition and the rate of growth*

At the end of the last chapter I tried to point out that insofar as — in a mental experiment — a country may proceed by starting from the same initial state on two paths, the growth rate of the aggregate index number of volume will be slower on the harmonic path than on the path of rush.

But now we do not intend to compare two hypothetical paths but to seek an answer to the following question: what is the effect of *transition* on the growth rate? From the logical aspect, this is a problem of a different nature. Namely, what happens if a country wants to shift from a forced growth path to the harmonic one? In such a case it does not simply choose the slower path but, for the time of transition, additional braking effects will be inevitable.

A simple argument: in the case of rush the country spends one per cent of GDP on road building, in the case of harmonic growth it will spend two per cent. But if it spent one per cent for two decades and wants to shift now to the harmonic path, it must, for a long time, spend *more* than two per cent, in order to 'catch up', to perform, in addition to the tasks which are due now, also those postponed. And road building belongs to the kind of investment where the output/capital ratio is particularly low. If, therefore, instead of the one per cent we spend now two and a half per cent on this target — instead of creating with these resources machine building plants where the output/capital ratio is high — the growth rate of production will no doubt slow down.

It is worth while in this context reflecting on some Hungarian data. Let us take the output/capital ratio of Hungarian industry and agriculture as the unit of measurement. (According to the terminology of Hungarian statistics: global domestic product in 1969, at 1968 prices divided by the gross value of fixed assets as of 1st January 1969, at 1968 prices*). This indicator has the value of 0.07 in water management,

---

* Source of the data is the publication (72) of the Central Statistical Office.

0.14 in transport and communications, and 0.04 in personal services and housing. Clearly, the greater the shift in investments towards the latter sectors, the more the *average* output/capital ratio of the national economy diminishes, that is, the growth rate would necessarily slow down.

The slowing down in the wake of the shift to the harmonic path is a *consequence,* not a target, nor a means. It is *not a target:* we do not slow down because we prefer a comfortable pace to a fast one. *Nor is it a means*: we would not achieve anything by merely slowing down the economy. If every activity were more lazily performed than before, we would not get nearer to harmony by a jot. Certain processes must be slowed down, others (e.g. the formation of consumption capital, the development of productive and service branches lagging behind) accelerated, that is, the activities and resources must, in the final analysis, be regrouped to some extent.

Is it absolutely certain that the growth of the aggregate indices of output will slow·down for the time of transition?

Making up for postponements and neglect will definitely act in the direction of deceleration, at least in the majority of fields. This effect can be more or less reliably foreseen and planned.

At the same time (and, to a considerable part, as an independent process) an improvement in efficiency can take place in our country. Under the heading of 'efficiency', similarly to section 5.1, many kinds of factors can be summed up: rationality of economic decisions, diligence of the workers and their work discipline, the orderly operation of economic life, etc. If all these improve, this works, of course, in the direction of increasing the aggregate indices of output. Elimination of disproportions, a more consistent meeting of the harmony requirements may contribute in themselves to increasing efficiency, although this contribution may assert itself at several removes and with a lag so that it is difficult to 'lay hands on'.

Of course, economic management must not passively look at the development of efficiency, but must promote improvement in several ways. The task of planning consists of participating in the elaboration of the necessary measures. It is, however, difficult to plan numerically, in a reliable manner, the anticipated effect of measures aimed at the improvement of efficiency.

In the final analysis, it is impossible to give an exact and unequivocal answer to the question concerning what the growth rate of the economy will be in the next fifteen years*. I will restrict myself to drawing up a few alternative prognoses:

(a) If we implement the transition to the harmonic path of growth with full consistency, and efficiency does not improve in the meantime in comparison to

---

* It was with justification that a study by G. Cukor (2) pointed out that the growth rate of the economy must not be listed among the tasks constituting a target, but the growth rate is one of the results of the plan-calculations aimed at the implementation of the plan objectives.

the earlier situation, the growth rate of the aggregate indices of output will considerable diminish.

(b) If we implement the transition to the harmonic growth path with full consistency but efficiency improves in the meantime palpably, this may more or less counterbalance the slowing effect of the transition. Some slowdown is probable even in this case: we can hardly expect a real acceleration in the rate of growth.

(c) For some time the present rate of growth may be maintained even without a considerable improvement in efficiency, if we continue to stay half-way between the harmonic path and rush, and even somewhat approach the latter. It is possible that this can be done even for fifteen years — but the consequences for the more distant future may be very grave indeed. It is, however, much more likely that this policy cannot be continued even in the next fifteen years without incurring great losses and shocks.

I, for one, would propose to discard alternative (c) and weigh in the course of long-term planning both alternatives (a) and (b). They reflect the same economic policy: a consistent transition to the harmonic path. They differ only in respect of the efficiency forecast: in this respect, however, it is justified to calculate more and less optimistic variants simultaneously.

When the ideas set out in this study were submitted to discussion, several people put the question: if we sincerely want to realize all the twelve requirements of harmony, does this not claim the quantity of resources which can only be created with a faster rate of growth? 'We rush towards the discarding of rush...'

The aphorism is witty — but erroneous. Transition cannot take place overnight. Tasks postponed and neglected for many years cannot be performed in a rush; transition is necessarily *gradual*. The past one and a half decades should be criticized not because there was a *gradual* shift from one path to the other, but because this movement was *inconsistent*.

It is quite possible that a complete transition cannot be brought about during a single fifteen-year period. All right, then let the period be 20 or 25 years. The essential thing is that *we should have definite ideas about the transition. Let us plan the gradual but consistent straightening of the front-line of economic progress; and let us fix a deadline for ourselves for completing the transition — even if this date is far away.*

I dare not represent this as a *general* standpoint which would be valid at all times and for every country. I have emphasized earlier that there may be external or internal circumstances justifying a rush. I believe, however, that in a socialist country like Hungary, at the level of moderate development that has been achieved, with the easier international situation prevailing in the early seventies, we may justifiably propose the consistent transition to the harmonic growth path.

6.4. Transition and the standard of living

It has also emerged from the discussions that some people are afraid the ideas exposed in the study would harm the standard of living of the population. My opponents in the debate argued as follows: we wish the standard of living to rise rapidly in Hungary. To this end it is indispensable that production should grow fast. Thus, if anybody objects to the high rate of growth, he is obstructing in the final analysis the intention of rapidly raising the standard of living.

This reasoning may be attacked on several points.

Above all: it tacitly assumes an unchanged proportion of consumption to investment, or even with a growing share of the latter. But this is not compulsory. The rate of investment is already high at present in the Hungarian economy. It is worth while thinking out — at least as one of the plan variants — the case in which, to a certain extent, a gradual shift takes place in favour of consumption. It is possible that this would even promote an improvement in the efficiency of investments. It seems that we can hardly provide sufficient organizing capacity and leading specialists to cope with the accelerating spread of investment activity*.

But let us now dismiss the proportion of consumption to investment. It is my conviction that the

---
* This is a phenomenon related to what is called by B. Horvat 'the investment absorptive capacity' of the system. See (27).

material satisfaction of the population, not to mention now the non-material factors influencing its well-being, is a function not only of the total volume of consumption, of the *consumption flow,* but of other effects as well:

How is the consumption *stock* developing? This is a problem, almost of equal rank with the classical dilemma of the proportion between consumption and investment, of what the proportion within total investment between the formation of productive and consumption capital will be.

When evaluating both the consumption flow and the consumption stock, not only its total volume but also its *composition* is decisive.

With all that I have no intention of underestimating the importance of the total volume of consumption, of the per capita consumption flow. It is no mere coincidence that I have listed its regular growth *as first* among the requirements of harmony. I do not propose, for the sake of any kind of 'adjustment of the front-line' that the growth of the consumption flow should be slower than what has been explained in the context of the requirement no. 1. That is, it should be at least 2-3 per cent on annual average for a long period, possible even more.

Suppose a choice had to be made between the following two alternatives:

First alternative: an annual 3 per cent growth of the consumption flow and, in the meantime, an ever fuller satisfaction of postponed and neglected requirements, a catching up in the formation of consumption capital; the development of better proportions between consumption flow and stock; an elimination of shortages.

Second alternative: an annual 5 per cent growth of the consumption flow and, in the meantime, further postponement of requirements already postponed and neglected; a continued lag in the formation of consumption capital; continued disproportions between the consumption flow and stock; persisting of the shortage phenomena.

I would choose the first alternative without hesitation. I believe, if the economic contents of the choice were sufficiently explained, the majority of the Hungarian population would take a similar stand.

When speaking about these two alternatives, we have already touched upon the subject of the next chapter: the phenomena of shortages, the problem of disequilibrium.

CHAPTER 7

DISEQUILIBRIUM

The first six chapters of my study have dealt with planning, with the formulation of economic policy. But, as a matter of fact, this is only the first half of the problem. The plans must also be implemented.

Though the majority of my study discusses planning, I would not like to overestimate the role of planning in the actual functioning of the economy. If we collate the results of the recently ended five-year plan period and of the one in process with the plans themselves, we will find that half-way between forced and harmonic growth the plan was nearer to harmony than its implementation.

The phenomena of rush is similar to the situation of a man wanting to abandon smoking: he again and again decides to give up smoking but still lights a cigarette in the end.

Limitations on the length of my study do not permit me to discuss the deviations between the plan and its implementation in a comprehensive manner. I will restrict myself to the examination of a few problems in chapters 7 and 8.

7.1. *The investment tension*

The most conspicuous form of repeated relapsing into the mistakes of rush is the 'running ahead' of investments*. The phenomenon can be directly observed in a *physical* form. On the one side, the *demand*, the necessary *inputs,* are determined by the investment decisions adopted. In the wake of the decision a series of material inputs becomes necessary: beginning with the designing-engineering activity, through the construction of the building to the domestic production or imports of machinery and their installation. On the other side the *possibilities* are given, the potential suited for turning out the *outputs* necessary for the implementation of the investments: the capacities of the building material industry, the construction industry, the designing institutes planning the projects, the limits of foreign exchange available for investment purposes, etc.

---

* On the tensions of the investment market see the articles by J. Drecin (14) and I. Berend (6). My attention has been drawn to important viewpoints relating to the subject in interviews with J. Drecin and G. Darvas (National Planning Office).

For a long time already, the demand for investment goods has been exceeding in Hungary the supply available for implementation. This disproportionality is called *investment tension*.

Up to now I have stressed the physical aspect of the disproportionality, although it naturally has *a financial* reflection as well. In earlier years this did not have too great a role. The bulk of investment decisions was taken centrally, the important products were allocated in physical terms. In recent years, however, particularly since the reform of economic control and management in 1968* the influence of the financial sphere has increased, among other things, on investment. Some investment decisions have become decentralized. The share of projects financed from the profit of state-owned or co-operative enterprises, or from the revenues of lower government bodies (e.g. of local councils), the savings of the population and with bank credits has increased. Investment tension in the financial sphere means, under our present conditions that the purchasing power oriented toward investment goods, the effective demand for investment goods and services is greater than their supply, calculated at valid prices. The excess demand on the market for investment goods pushes up prices. Though government

---

* The literature describing and evaluating the reform (with foreign-language editions among them) is rich indeed. Some works which provide general orientation: R. Nyers (55), (56), (57), I. Friss, ed. (20) and T. Nagy (49).

price control makes efforts to put a brake on that, the rise in prices still asserts itself.

Demand for investments is increased by several forces. The process begins even in the planning phase. When the five-year plan now under implementation was drawn up, it was initially intended to raise the total volume of investments by 6-7 per cent annually. There were intermediate variants of the plan which aimed at increased self-restraint and provided for a 4 per cent target. The figure in the final document was 5 per cent. This is not low, yet those drawing up the plan were almost ashamed and excused themselves for it. But plan-implementation overbid them and realized more investments.

The central investment decisions are frequently overambitious. In addition, the 'pressure from below' is extremely strong. The necessity, the undelayable nature of every investment action is supported by a legion of arguments. Frequently, however, the economic leadership is faced with unalterable facts instead of arguments; the local leaders make promises and the government is compelled to fulfil them with investments. There is another factor: the problem of investments financed from local (self-government or enterprise) revenues. When drawing up the plans, the starting assumption was that enterprise profits (and similarly, the tax and other revenues of the bodies of local self-government) will be of average level. When the revenue is higher than average, a greater amount of investments is started than planned. If, however, it is smaller than expected, investments are not stopped or slowed down, but central support is urgently asked for to complete the original plan.

Thus, the situation develops in a rather paradoxical manner. The central organs of the state cannot look on passively while, for lack of financial resources, some project started remains *incomplete*. But, among other things, it is precisely this interference, the central help and credit provided indiscriminately that leads to investment tension, to queueing up for investment goods and services, to material and labour shortages, to the protraction of investment actions, that is, in the final analysis, to the swelling of the stock of *incomplete* investments.

7.2. 'Suction'

The disproportion dominating the investment market is the kernel, the starting point of a broader group of phenomena: the **general disequilibrium between demand and supply**. The market of investment goods is, namely, not delimited from the market of inputs necessary for current production of non-investment character, nor from that of consumer goods. Those commissioning the building of a factory or a residental building compete for the capacity of the same building material industry and the same construction industry. With the same foreign exchange we can import productive machinery or radio sets, clothes or perfumes.

But it is not only investors who stand in queues in Hungary. There are shortages also in other fields. In current production the shortage of materials, spare-parts and intermediary products, labour and foreign exchange frequently cause difficulties. And consumers are queueing up for flats, cars and telephone extensions. It often occurs that the global supply available from a major group of consumer goods is sufficient, but there is an annoying shortage of concrete products, sizes, or types within a group.

True, in Hungary the situation in the consumer goods' market has much inproved in recent years. A look at the shop-windows is enough to substantiate this. Supply of staple foodstuffs and mass consumer goods is smooth. The supply of commodities has been expanded both by the development of domestic production and by imports. Development can be explained by several factors: by the effect of the reform of the economic mechanism, by deliberate central measures and interference in the interest of smooth supply and, in general, by the public spirit predominant in Hungarian economic life which deems that the satisfaction of the consumers is of prime importance.

Yet, however considerable the results are, it would be too early to state that we have succeeded in eliminating shortages from every field of consumption, not to speak of the tensions mentioned in the market for producer and investment goods. Beyond that, at this place in my study I would not restrict myself exclusively to the analysis of the present Hungarian situation, but would like to speak *in more general terms* about shortage phenomena and their interrelation with the problems of rush that are similarly more general in character and appear not merely in present-day Hungary.

These phenomena have already been given many names. In German literature we find the name 'Mangelwirtschaft', 'shortage economy'. Traditional price theory and equilibrium theory simply calls it excess demand. Others use the expression 'sellers' market', emphasizing with it that in this case of disequilibrium the seller dominates the market and the buyer is at his mercy, as opposed to the 'buyers' market', where the situation would be the reverse.

The author has recently written a book under the title of *Anti-Equilibrium*, one of the major subjects of which is market disequilibrium. In my book I call the state of general (or very broad) shortage: 'suction'. In such cases the buyer thirstily sucks the goods towards himself; as opposed to the situation of 'pressure' where the seller presses his goods on to the buyer*.

I would like to avoid repetition of what is in the book. I shall, therefore, not describe suction in detail, nor deal comprehensively with its causes and effects. I

---

* See (42), (43). In my book I give my detailed reasons why I feel it necessary to introduce new terminology; how the states of 'pressure' and 'suction' differ from what the neoclassical price theory calls excess supply and excess demand.

shall touch upon the problem only insofar as it is linked to the main subject of my study: rush and harmonic growth.

We have here two, conceptually distinct groups of phenomena. *'Rush' is a possible path of economic growth.* If we wish to state whether a country is running this path, we have to consider in turn several fields of economic and social life. (See the twelve requirements of harmony.) *'Suction' is, however, a characteristic state of the market, a type of market disequilibrium.*

Though the two are conceptually distinct notions, historically they usually go hand in hand. *'Rush' and 'suction' can be traced back to a considerable extent, to common motives, they mutually reinforce each other and even the direction of their effects coincides.*

Let us start with *motivation*. The starting point for market disequilibrium, as emphasized at the beginning of this chapter, is tension on the investment market. The source of this is, in general, the same as that of rush: the expansive efforts prevailing in the economy, the demand for impatient running ahead.

The two groups of phenomena are interrelated in the *financial sphere*. Rush claims great investments. Its financing takes place partly in an inflationary manner: purchasing power swells. On the other hand, government price control puts a brake on the rise in prices. Repressed inflation then leads to excess demand, to 'suction'.

Finally, it is perhaps the most important interrelation that *'suction' is the precursor of 'rush'*, the environment where 'rush' can lastingly prevail. If 'pressure' prevailed on the market, the producers would have to turn out what the users really ask for. This would, to some extent, force the producers to develop a production and consumption pattern which the user, the consumer, the buyer feels harmonic. In the case of *general* pressure, the disturbances of adaptation immediately appear in the form of swelling stocks and in sudden shifts of relative prices.

The situation is different in the case of 'suction'. A general shortage of commodities clears the market more safely than the most flexible system of prices: the buyer buys anything, because he is glad to get any commodity at all. He cannot object to either the poor range of choice, or poor quality, but must accept what he gets.

It follows from what has been said that the market situation is a good way of telling to what extent the effort at liquidating rush is consistent. The successes achieved in the consumer goods market indicate that in this respect, too, we came closer to the harmonic path of growth. However, as long as in major fields investment tension, suction, disequilibrium persist, we are at most half-way between forcing the rate of growth and harmony, but we have not yet consistently taken the path to harmonic growth.

7.3. Digression: polemics with the theory of 'unbalanced growth'

I should like to enter here into argument with the adherents of 'unbalanced growth'*. Before writing this study I re-read some of their major works. It was a queer feeling for a *Hungarian* economist. Every phenomenon that annoys and even enrages the Hungarian employee charged with procuring materials, or the housewife, is praised in these works. The theory of 'unbalanced growth' is the glorification of suction.

I would not like to discard their principles unconditionally in the case of every country or regarding every development period of all countries. E.g. Hirschmann is under the influence of his experiences in Columbia. I have not yet been there. Maybe suction exerts a propelling force in a sleepy country. Investment is too small; there are too few enterprising people to organize economic activity; there is too little incentive for investment activity. In such cases a shortage situation may have advantages. It becomes profitable for enterprises to satisfy the shortage quickly. The protest emerging in the wake of shortages exerts political pressure on the government bodies and institutions, urging government interference.

It is thought-provoking whether a general shortage situation is not an indispensable force (or at least a

---

* Its most important representatives are: Hirschmann (25) and Streeten (64).

very efficient one) for providing the impetus to the 'take-off' at the historical moment when a country, which has stagnated or has just been bumping along up to now, must be pushed to the path of fast growth. Maybe, looking back from a historical perspective, we shall acknowledge this historical role of suction at the time of 'take-off'.

Today, however, we here in Hungary have certainly left this period behind us. Our problem is not sleepiness but insomnia. It is therefore my conviction that, under the given Hungarian conditions, when working on the plans of the next fifteen years, it would be a mistake to adopt the theory of 'unbalanced growth'.

7.4. Reserves and adaptation

After the polemic, let us return to the positive explanation.

All that has been said about the relation between market disequilibrium and forced growth is, in the final analysis, related to harmony-requirement no. 12, the continuous care for reserves. 'Suction' means the lack of reserves, while 'pressure' means the creation of reserves in every sphere of production and turnover. A state, where the producer feels that regarding his possibilities he could, as a matter of fact, produce even more: the capacity, material stocks, and labour are available, and he is constrained only by marketability. This feeling compels him to find out the desires of the buyer, to create — with the introduction of new products — new needs and thus new markets.

The formation of reserves begins with investment resources. Thus we have come back to where we started the analysis of disequilibrium: to investment tension.

The present practice is that the plan allocates, to the last penny, the investment funds among the planned users. In the course of implementation it then turns out: first, that everything costs more than originally forecast, partly owing to price rises, partly because the actual real inputs were underestimated. And it also turns out that even such investments are indispensable as did not figure in the plan. It is enough to insert these into the programme (while the planned investments are continued) and the investment tension has already appeared.

As a matter of fact, everybody acknowledges that it is not correct to allocate the whole investment fund in advance, but that some reserves are needed. Only the size of the reserve is debated. Many are inclined to say that only a reserve of 1-2-3 per cent is needed. In my opinion, what is necessary is greater *by an order of magnitude*: 10-20 or 30 per cent is needed, not 1-2 or 3. Of course, the volume of the reserves, of the unallocated resources is not independent of the plan horizon: much more is needed for fifteen years than for five, and a more modest reserve will do for next year.

Behind the allocation of investment funds in

advance there looms, as a matter of fact, a problem of 'plan philosophy'. How far does the wisdom of planners reach? Where is the limit to foresight? He who allocates everything in advance, he cannot be taken by any surprise on the way. However, he who puts aside great reserves believes that it is already a great achievement if processes are planned in advance to 70-80-90 per cent; to trust in a more exact foresight would be self-deception. *Life must be permitted to complement — and adjust, if necessary — the plan. For that, however, actual material investment resources, mobile capital is needed.*

When talking about the problem with some practical planners I have repeatedly experienced that it is almost inconceivable for them that a medium or long-term plan *should provide for an excess supply of investment goods*. They brought forward all kinds of other solutions just to circumvent this. E.g. some of them proposed to build up the plan on fundamentally pessimistic prognoses and if things turned out more favourable than prognosticated, the surplus should be declared a reserve. Or: the planned investment actions should be ranked by importance. If resources turned out to be too scarce, the actions on the bottom of the list could be omitted. Though these are remarkable ideas, yet, in my opinion, they do not solve the problem. The ideas mentioned keep in view, namely, that aspect of the reserves which is related to *uncertainty*: what should we do if the situation turns out less favourably than according to optimistic (or average, not too pessimistic) expectation. But this is not the most important aspect of the problem. *The most important one is that with a disequilibrium of the opposite sign new power relations should be established on the investment market.* The producers of investment goods should compete for the commissions, and the investment decision-makers should compete to attract the innovator with his initiative and ideas.

One of the phenomena accompanying rush is rigidity, bureaucratic cramp. 'We cannot change this, a resolution has already been passed...' or 'This was not contained in the plan, there is no material cover for it, we shall try to fit it in when compiling the next plan.' Under such conditions we perceive some serious shift in needs in vain, it is impossible to adjust quickly. In vain does an innovator appear with a major invention — if its introduction is capital intensive, a deaf ear is turned to him and implementation is put off. *Quick adaptation of the system can be made possible only by liquidating the tension due to shortage, with major reserves (within that, with mobile real capital suited to the quick implementation of investments, with the excess supply of investment goods).*

And with this I have come to the last subject of my study: to the relation between the plan and the market.

CHAPTER 8

EFFECT OF THE PLAN AND THE MARKET ON THE HARMONY OF GROWTH

8.1. Division of labour

We may meet with the following view:

The *cause* of rush is planning itself. Only planning can deliberately deviate from the proportions which, if left alone, would nicely develop by themselves under the influence of the market. You need not travel to Chicago to hear this opinion, there are people in Budapest who believe it.

I for one, cannot accept this standpoint. Truly harmonic growth is promoted by clever planning.

The first group of arguments is related to the fact that *part of the harmony-requirements can by no means assert themselves 'spontaneously', exclusively under the effect of the market.*

Infringement upon requirement no. 2 (harmonic

satisfaction of consumer needs), no. 6 (education), no. 8.3 (research) and no. 11 (protection of nature) appears in several fields as a so-called 'externality'*. The market does not deter unfavourable externalities and does not stimulate favourable ones — for that deliberate interference is needed.

The market does not automatically ensure satisfaction of requirement no. 4.1, full employment. Since Keynes, this is a trivial truth, irrespective of political adherence, for every economist.

A whole series of 'humanitarian' harmony-requirements fall beyond the scope of the market: requirement no. 3 (an equitable distribution of income), no. 4.2 (protection of health), no. 4.3 (care for old people), no. 4.4 (public security) and requirement no. 5 (the possibility for the free evolution of talents).

Another group of arguments starts from the *practical advantages of foresight*. According to a Hungarian proverb, 'a wise man learns from the mistakes of others'. He who relies exclusively on the market, wishes to learn merely from his own domestic experience, ex post. If the market signals, with its particular system of signals, the shifts in relative prices and profits, then (but only then) the proportions are changed. But why should we wait as long as that?

---

* Externalities are effects which are not (or not sufficiently) reflected in prices and costs — that is, in the final analysis, in the *money* accounts of the enterprise or the households. E.g. the factory makes noise, disturbs the population living in its environment, but does not 'pay' for it, it does not burden the budged of the enterprise.

History has created a particular situation: about a hundred and fifty countries live side by side, on very different levels of development. Apart from the richest countries at the head of the list, the others can learn from the experiences of those preceding them, both from the good and the bad experiences. One of the fundamental tasks of long-term planning is to collect these experiences systematically, analyse them and, considering these as well as the different government normative requirements, to take a *preliminary* decision on the development of harmonic proportions.

Of course, this does not mean elimination of the market. In several parts of my study I have already touched upon the subject in other contexts. First I have stressed when defining the notion of harmony in an abstract manner: the growth path is subject to control by the population. Only what has been accepted by the population without protest can be considered as harmonic. The market is necessary as a relatively shock-free 'mild' forum of approval or protest.

Later, in section 7.4 it has been mentioned that great scope for movement must be left in the plans for life to complement and adjust the plan. In other words, this means that the market has been given a possibility to function as a tool for correcting the plan. To a considerable part, the market must dispose of the investment reserves, mobile real capital which has not been allocated in detail in the plan. The existence of the uncommitted liquid investment reserve, mobile real capital, is at least as important a *physical* condition of the effective functioning of the market and of its playing a particular role in complementing and adjusting the plans, as the *legal and institutional* conditions authorizing enterprise autonomy.

8.2. Interrelation of reforms and change

In the last one and a half decades deep-reaching changes have taken place in the Hungarian economy and the long-term plan envisages further changes. The changes are diversified, yet they can be summed up in four major trends:

(1) The economic policy related to growth is changing. We are in the process of transition to a harmonic path.

(2) The general situation of the market is changing. Initial steps have been taken, for the time being, mainly on the consumer goods' market, to eliminate suction and to liquidate shortage phenomena.

(3) Institutional forms are changing. The system of short-term plan instructions has been liquidated, the autonomy of enterprises has increased, together with the growing role of the price mechanism, of the profit motive and of the market processes.

(4) The methods of planning are changing. Mathematical planning has appeared. Instead of the meticulous and shortsighted planning of details, the

long-term planning concentrating on major processes has come to the fore. The short-term national economic plan is no longer broken down to enterprises.

These four kinds of changes are closely interrelated. My study has not given by any means an exhaustive survey of these interrelations since it has dealt mainly with the first process, but it has frequently referred to the mutual relations. *The more consistently each of these processes materializes, taken separately, the more it promotes also the advance of the other three.*

We, who are cultivating theoretical economics, have not yet really understood these processes and their mutual relations. In many a question we are still relying on a hunch; we must still discuss these problems at length. And I hope this study will contribute to the final clarification — if not with finished mature statements, at least by stimulating discussion.

REFERENCES

(1) ADELMAN, I. and C.T. MORRIS: 'Factor analysis of the interrelationship between social and political variables and per capita gross national product'. *Quarterly Journal of Economics*, 79 (1965) 555-578.
(2) ADELMAN, I. and C.T. MORRIS: 'An econometric model of socio-economic and political change in underdeveloped countries'. *American Economic Review*, 58 (1968) 1184-1218.
(3) AUGUSTINOVICS, M.: 'A hosszutávu tervezés módszertanához' (Contribution to the methodology of longterm planning). *Közgazdasági Szemle*, 16 (1969) 1168-1178.
(4) AUGUSTINOVICS, M.: 'A hosszutávu tervezés kvantifikálásáról' (On the quantification of long-term planning). *Közgazdasági Szemle*, 16 (1969) 1269-1281.
(5) BEKKER, ZS.: 'Néhány gondolat Magyarország gépiparának fejlődéséről' (Some ideas about the development of the Hungarian engineering industry). *Közgazdasági Szemle*, 17 (1970) 1033-1048.
(6) BEREND, I.: 'A beruházási piac helyzetéről' (On the situation of the investment market). *Közgazdasági Szemle*, 17 (1970) 140-154.
(7) BRÓDY, A.: Érték és ujratermelés. Budapest: Közgazdasági és Jogi Könyvkiadó (1969). For translation see (8).
(8) BRÓDY, A.: *Proportions, Prices and Planning.* Budapest — Amsterdam: Publishing House of the Hungarian Academy of Sciences — North-Holland Publishing Company (1970).
(9) CASS, D.: 'Optimum growth in an aggregative model of capital accumulation: a turnpike theorem'. *Econometrica*, 34 (1966) 833-850.

(10) CHENERY, H.B.: 'Pattern of industrial growth'. *American Economic Review*, 50 (1960) 624-654.
(11) CRAVERO, R., G. BARNA, Á. KISS, I. MONIGL and J. NAGY: *Az oktatás távlati fejlesztési koncepciója* (Long-term development conception of education; mimeographed). Budapest: Munkaerő és Életszinvonal Távlati Tervezési Bizottság (1971).
(12) CUKOR, G.: *Hosszutávu tervezés az iparban* (Long-term planning in industry; manuscript). Budapest: MTA Közgazdaságtudományi Intézete (1970).
(13) DORFMAN, R., P.A. SAMUELSON and R.M. SOLOW: *Linear Programming and Economic Analysis*. New York — Toronto — London: McGraw-Hill (1958).
(14) DRECIN, J.: 'Beruházási egyensuly, irányitási és döntési mechanizmus' (Investment equilibrium, mechanisms of control and decision). *Társadalmi Szemle*, 26 (1971) No. 6. 3-13.
(15) EHRLICH, É.: 'An examination of the interrelation between consumption indicators expressed in physical units and per capita national income'. *Czechoslovak Economic Papers* (1966) No. 7. 109-136.
(16) EHRLICH, E.: 'International comparisons by indicators expressed in physical units'. *Acta Oeconomica*, 2 (1967) 107-148.
(17) EHRLICH, É.: 'Nemzetközi elemzések a magyar távlati tervezéshez'. *Országos Tervhivatal Tervgazdasági Intézet Közleményei* (1968) No.2., A. füzet. For translation see (18).
(18) EHRLICH, É.: *International analyses to be used in Hungarian long-term planning, Volume 'A'* (mimeographed). Budapest: Institute of Economic Planning of the Hungarian Planning Office (1968).

(19) EHRLICH, É.: 'Nemzeti jövedelmek dinamikus nemzetközi öszszehasonlitása naturális mutatókkal' (Dynamic international comparison of national incomes with the aid of physical indicators). *Közgazdasági Szemle*, 15 (1968) 191-212.
(20) FRISS, I. (ed.): *Reform of the Economic Mechanism in Hungary*. Budapest: Akadémiai Kiadó (1969).
(21) HAHN, F.H. and R.C.O. MATTHEWS: 'The theory of economic growth: A survey'. *Economic Journal*, 74 (1964) 779-903.
(22) HETÉNYI, I.: 'Gazdasági fejlődés és hosszutávu tervezés'. *Gazdaság*, 2 (1968) No.4. 7-17. For translation see (23).
(23) HETÉNYI, I.: 'Economic development and long-term planning'. *Acta Oeconomica*, 4 (1969) 155-168.
(24) HETÉNYI, I.: 'A hosszutávu tervezés kérdéséhez' (On the problems of long-term planning). *Társadalmi Szemle*, 25 (1970) No.10. 12-24.
(25) HIRSCHMAN, A.O.: *The Strategy of Economic Development*. New Haven: Yale University Press (1958).
(26) HOFFMANN, W.G.: 'Prosperity goods in the growth process'. *The German Economic Review*, 9 (1971) 1-10.
(27) HORVAT, B.: 'The optimum rate of investment'. *Economic Journal*, 68 (1958) 747-767.
(28) HOUTHAKKER, H.S.: 'The present state of consumption theory'. *Econometrica*, 29 (1961) 704-740.
(29) HUSZÁR, I., R. HOCH, J. KOVÁCS and J. TIMÁR (eds.): *Az életszinvonal alakulása Magyarországon* (Development of living standards in Hungary). Budapest: Munkaerő és Életszinvonal Távlati Tervezési Bizottság (1969).

(30) HUSZÁR, I., R. HOCH, J. KOVÁCS and J. TIMÁR: 'Hipotézisek a foglalkoztatás és az életszinvonal alakulására Magyarországon 1985-ig' (Hypotheses about the development of employment and living standards in Hungary). *Gazdaság*, 3 (1969) No.3. 17-41.

(31) JÁNOSSY, F.: *A gazdasági fejlettség mérhetősége és uj mérési módszere* (Measurability of the economic development level and a new method for its measurement). Budapest: Közgazdasági és Jogi Könyvkiadó (1963).

(32) JÁNOSSY, F.: *A gazdasági fejlődés trendvonala és a helyreállitási periódusok* (The trend line of economic development and the reconstruction periods). Budapest: Közgazdasági és Jogi Könyvkiadó (1966).

(33) JÁNOSSY, F.: *Das Ende der Wirtschaftswunder — Erscheinung und Wesen der Wirtschaftlichen Entwicklung.* Frankfurt: Neue Kritik (1971).

(34) JÁNOSSY, F.: 'Gazdaságunk mai ellentmondásainak eredete és felszámolásuk utja' (The origin of present contradictions in the Hungarian economy and the way to eliminate them). *Közgazdasági Szemle*, 16 (1969) 806-829.

(35) KISS, Á. and J. TIMÁR: 'Szakemberellátás és munkaerőstruktura' (Supply of qualified labour and manpower structure). *Társadalmi Szemle*, (1970) No.6. 25-38.

(36) KISS, Á. and J. TIMÁR: 'A munkaerő-struktura és az oktatás fejlesztése (Manpower structure and the development of education). *Társadalmi Szemle*, 25 (1970) No.7. 16-24.

(37) KISS Á. and J. TIMÁR: 'The supply of qualified manpower — Labour force structure — Education'. *Acta Oeconomica*, 6 (1971) 201-218.

(38) KOOPMANS, T.C.: 'Objectives, constraints and outcomes in optimal growth models'. *Econometrica*, 35 (1967) 1-15.
(39) KORNAI, J.: *A gazdasági szerkezet matematikai tervezése.* Budapest: Közgazdasági és Jogi Könyvkiadó (1965). For translation see (40).
(40) KORNAI, J.: *Mathematical Planning of Structural Decisions.* Amsterdam — Budapest: North-Holland Publishing Company — Publishing House of the Hungarian Academy of Sciences (1967).
(41) KORNAI, J.: *The Place of Mathematical Planning in the Control of the Economic Systems* (mimeographed). Geneva: United Nations Economic Commission for Europe (1970).
(42) KORNAI, J.: *Anti-Equilibrium.* Budapest: Közgazdasági és Jogi Könyvkiadó (1971). For translation see (43).
(43) KORNAI, J.: *Anti-Equilibrium.* Amsterdam: North-Holland Publishing Company (1971).
(44) KOVÁCS, J.: *Szakképzés és népgazdaság* (Vocational training and the national economy). Budapest: Közgazdasági és Jogi Könyvkiadó (1968).
(45) LIST, F.: *Das nationale System der Politischen Ökonomie.* Basel — Tübingen: Kyklos — Mohr (1959).
(46) MALINVAUD, E. and M.O.L. BACHARACH (eds.): *Activity Analysis in the Theory of Growth and Planning.* London — Melbourne — Toronto — New York: Macmillan — St Martin's Press (1967).
(47) MCKENZIE, L.: 'Turnpike theorems for a generalized Leontief model'. *Econometrica*, 31 (1963) 165-180.
(48) MCKENZIE L.: 'Maximal paths in the Von Neumann Model'. In (45), 43-63.

(49) NAGY, T.: 'The Hungarian economic reform, past and future'. *American Economic Review, Papers and Proceedings*, 61 (1971) 430-436.
(50) NEUMANN, J. VON: 'A model of general economic equilibrium'. *Review of Economic Studies*, 13 (1945) 1-9.
(51) NEUMANN, J. VON: 'Az általános gazdasági egyensuly egy modellje'. In (52), 160-176. Translation of (50).
(52) NEUMANN, J. VON: *Válagatott elödások és tanulmányok* (Selected lectures and studies). Budapest: Közgazdasági és Jogi Könyvkiadó (1965).
(53) NURKSE, R.: *Problems of Capital Formation in Underdeveloped Countries*. Oxford: Blackwell (1955).
(54) NURKSE, R.: *Equilibrium and Growth in the World Economy*. Cambridge, Mass.: Harvard University Press (1961).
(55) NYERS, R.: *Gazdaságpolitikánk és a gazdasági mechanizmus reformja* (Economic policy and the reform of the economic mechanism in Hungary). Budapest: Kossuth (1968).
(56) NYERS, R.: *25 kérdés és válasz gazdaságpolitikai kérdésekről.* Budapest: Kossuth (1969). For translation see (57).
(57) NYERS, R.: *Economic Reform in Hungary: Twenty-five Questions and Twenty-five Answers*. Budapest: Pannonia Press (1969).
(58) RADNER, R.: 'Paths of economic growth that are optimal with regard only to final states: A 'turnpike theorem'. *Review of Economic Studies*, 28 (1961) 98-104.
(59) RAMSEY, F.P.: 'A mathematical theory of saving'. *Economic Journal*, 38 (1928) 543-559.

(60) RIMLER, J.: 'A gazdasági fejlodés vizsgálata és a faktoranalizis' (The examination of economic growth and factor analysis). *Közgazdasági Szemle*, 17 (1970) 913-926.
(61) RIMLER, J.: 'Kisérlet a faktoranalizis alkalmazására a gazdasági fejlődés vizsgálatában' (An attempt at applying factor analysis to the investigation of economic growth). *Közgazdasági Szemle*, 17 (1970) 1195-1214.
(62) ROMÁN, Z.: 'Iparunk ágazati szerkezetének sajátosságai' (Particular features of the branch-pattern of Hungarian industry). *Közgazdasági Szemle* ,15 (1968) 1141-1153.
(63) ROSENSTEIN-RODAN, P.N.: 'Problems of industrialization of Eastern and South-Eastern Europe'. *Economic Journal*, 33 (1943).
(64) STREETEN, P.: 'Unbalanced growth'. *Oxford Economic Papers*, New Series, 11 (1959) 167-190.
(65) TSUKUI, J.: 'Turnpike theorem in a generalized dynamic input—output system'. *Econometrica*, 34 (1966) 396-407.
(66) YOUNG A.A.: Increasing returns and economic progress'. *Economic Journal*, 38 (1928) 527-542.
(67) *A magyar ipar ágazati szerkezete* (The branch-pattern of Hungarian industry). Budapest: Magyar Tudományos Akadémia Ipargazdaságtani Kutatócsoportja (1968).
(68) *A munkaerö és életszinvonal távlati tervkoncepciója* (The long-term planning conception of manpower and living standards; mimeographed). Budapest: Munkaerö és Eletszinvonal Távlati Tervezési Bizottság (1971).
(69) *A Study of Industrial Growth*. New York: United Nations (1963).
(70) *Az épitöipar nemzetközi fejlödésének elemzése* (Analysis of the international development of the construction industry; mimeographed). Budapest: Epitésgazdasági és Szervezési Intézet (1968).

(71) *Measuring the Nation's Wealth — Volume Twenty-Nine.* New York — Londen: Columbia University Press (1964).

(72) *Népgazdasági mérlegek 1960-70* (Balances of the national economy covering 1960-70). Budapest: Központi Statisztikai Hivatal (1971).